The Teaching of Ethics IX

Ethics in the Undergraduate Curriculum

Bernard Rosen
Arthur L. Caplan

INSTITUTE OF
SOCIETY, ETHICS AND
THE LIFE
SCIENCES THE
HASTINGS
CENTER

The Hastings Center
Institute of Society, Ethics and the Life Sciences
360 Broadway
Hastings-on-Hudson, New York 10706

Library of Congress Cataloging in Publication Data

Rosen, Bernard.
    Ethics in the undergraduate curriculum.
    (The Teaching of ethics ; 9)
    Bibliography: p.
    1. Ethics—Study and teaching (Higher)
I. Caplan, Arthur L., joint author. II. Title.
III. Series: Teaching of ethics ; 9.
BJ66.R67   170′.7′11   80–12351
ISBN 0–916558–13–4

Printed in the United States of America

Contents

FOREWORD

A concern for the ethical instruction and formation of students has always been a part of American higher education. Yet that concern has by no means been uniform or free of controversy. The centrality of moral philosophy in the undergraduate curriculum during the mid-nineteenth century gave way later during that century to the first signs of increasing specialization of the disciplines. By the middle of the twentieth century, instruction in ethics had, by and large, become confined almost exclusively to departments of philosophy and religion. Efforts to introduce ethics teaching in the professional schools and elsewhere in the university often met with indifference or outright hostility.

The past decade has seen a remarkable resurgence of interest in the teaching of ethics at both the undergraduate and professional school levels. Beginning in 1977, The Hastings Center, with the support of the Rockefeller Brothers Fund and the Carnegie Corporation of New York, undertook a systematic study of the teaching of ethics in American higher education. Our concern focused on the extent and quality of that teaching, and on the main possibilities and problems posed by widespread efforts to find a more central and significant role for ethics in the curriculum.

As part of that project, a number of papers, studies, and monographs were commissioned. Moreover, in an attempt to gain some degree of consensus, the authors of those studies worked together as a group for a period of two years. The study presented here represents one outcome of the project. We hope and believe it will be helpful for those concerned to advance and deepen the teaching of ethics in higher education.

Daniel Callahan   Sissela Bok
Project Co-Directors
The Hastings Center
Project on the Teaching of Ethics

About the Authors

Bernard Rosen

Bernard Rosen is an associate professor of philosophy at Ohio State University. He received his B.A. from Wayne State University and his Ph.D. in philosophy from Brown University. He is the author of a recent book, *Strategies of Ethics*.

Arthur L. Caplan

Arthur Caplan is Associate for the Humanities at The Hastings Center and Associate for Social Medicine in the Department of Medicine, College of Physicians and Surgeons, Columbia University. He did his undergraduate work at Brandeis University and received his Ph.D. in philosophy from Columbia University. Dr. Caplan was the recipient of an NEH post-doctoral fellowship for the year of 1976–77. He is the editor of *The Sociobiology Debate,* Harper & Row, 1978, and, the forthcoming *Concepts of Health and Disease in Medicine,* Addison-Wesley, 1980. He has contributed numerous articles to professional journals in the areas of ethics, medical ethics, and philosophy of science.

Introduction

More than one cultural commentator has claimed that the 1970s was "the age of ethics." Whether this is true or not, there developed an enormous amount of interest in ethics on college campuses. This interest manifested itself in many ways: in the variety of new ethics courses that were added to the curriculum; in the increase in symposia and colloquia concerning ethical themes and problems; in the number of new books and anthologies about applied ethics. It also appeared in the rise of subfields such as bioethics, environmental ethics, science and society; in the many recent inclusions of ethical and value requirements in the undergraduate curriculum; and in the shift in faculty research interests toward subjects that are largely concerned with ethics and values. The interest in ethics was not, however, confined to academia. A great deal of public attention was given to discussions of moral and value problems that arose in contemporary life and public policy. All of this activity has resulted in a significant change in the way ethics is taught to undergraduates. Our reason for writing this monograph is to describe, analyze, and reflect upon some of these changes.

The increase in ethics and values teaching in undergraduate institutions has raised a series of important concerns about how ethics and values should be taught. Central among these concerns are the problems of who is qualified to teach an ethics course, what the goals of an ethics course should be, how one defines the scope of an ethics course, how ethics courses can be evaluated, whether students have the capacity to learn about ethical and value issues by the time they arrive at a college, and what the content of courses on ethics and values should be. None of these concerns are new. However, shifts—both within the humanities departments, where ethics courses have traditionally been taught—and in those areas new to the teaching of ethics, have forced the teachers of ethics courses (and the appropriate administrators) to take a long and serious look at these concerns.

It is not our intention to pass judgment on the quality or importance of any given course on ethics and values. Rather, we shall try systematically to describe the various trends and patterns that have emerged in the past decade in the area of ethics teaching, and to try to highlight some of the central issues and problems that have resulted from this expansion of interest. We are surprised that the marked increase in the teaching of ethics has not brought forth an abundance of comment and analysis, given that it is such an important trend in higher education in America. Our hope is that, if this monograph does nothing else, it will stimulate the kind of critical attention that this new educational interest in the teaching of ethics surely deserves.

It does not take a detailed examination of the present state of ethics teaching in American colleges and universities to reveal that there is an enormous amount of activity going on in its name. There are many different courses or parts of courses taught by a variety of people in many different departments to all sorts of students for a variety of reasons. For example, there is a number of courses in subjects such as biology, social science, and political science in which significant portions of the course are devoted to considerations of ethical or valuational topics. Our solution to the methodological question of how to study such a broad and varied phenomenon has been to focus for the most part on those courses and teaching activities that are explicitly and primarily devoted to the teaching of ethics and values. This is not because ethics and values teaching can only go on in courses that have this avowed goal as their intention. Instead, it is because the task of investigating the entire range of activities in all course offerings within the undergraduate curriculum is simply beyond the capacities and expertise of the authors. Thus, our aim will be to delineate and describe the nature of teaching activities in the area of ethics in those courses, programs, and books that are explicitly and primarily aimed at this end.

We have organized the monograph around three major themes. The first third consists of an investigation of perceptions of what the teaching of ethics should be, with the addition of descriptive information about what the state of the teaching of ethics currently is. To help understand how the current situation has evolved, we present a brief discussion of the history of undergraduate ethics teaching prior to this decade. The second part of the monograph deals with a number of substantive issues in the actual teaching of ethics courses. We shall address such concerns as the goals of ethics courses, how to achieve successful instruction in ethics without becoming engaged in a process of indoctrination, the proper qualifications for ethics teachers, and the proper modes of evaluation and assessment of ethics courses. Our final section focuses on a number of practical pedagogical issues in teaching ethics courses to undergraduates. We are particularly interested in pinpointing some of the key issues that arise in the undergraduate classroom. That section, thus, will touch upon such topics as how one goes about dealing with various student objections to the enterprise of ethics, the question of how one deals with political issues in the classroom, novel modes of teaching ethics, and some interesting classroom techniques that have proven successful in the teaching of ethics to undergraduates.

I. General Background and Empirical Information

A. Recent History of Undergraduate Ethics Teaching

While moral philosophy has always been a part of American higher education, its importance and prestige have waxed and waned over the decades. Reflecting the influence of the English and Scottish universities, as well as the earlier history of the medieval university, the first American colleges gave a prominent place to ethics in the curriculum. The importance of moral philosophy became even more pronounced during the nineteenth century. As Douglas Sloan has noted:

> Throughout most of the nineteenth century, the most important course in the college curriculum was moral philosophy, taught usually by the college president and required of all senior students. The moral philosophy course was regarded as the capstone of the curriculum. It aimed to pull together, to integrate, and to give meaning and purpose to the students' entire college experience and course of study. In so doing it even more importantly also sought to equip the graduating seniors with the ethical sensitivity and insight needed if they were to put their newly acquired college education to use in ways that would benefit not only themselves and their own personal advancement, but the larger society as well.[1]

It was not simply that moral philosophy was thought to be an important subject. It was seen as the key to a view of higher education that stressed the importance of the moral formation of students within a fully unified curriculum. The intellectual unity of the curriculum was seen as a safeguard against cultural and moral chaos and as necessary for students to provide society with virtuous leadership. Beyond those cultural and civic purposes, moral philosophy was believed to be solidly founded on the nature of reality:

> Just as science was thought to reveal the divine handiwork in nature, so moral philosophy demonstrated moral purpose and design in human affairs. The moral law was considered to be as real and as inexorable as the law of gravity and both pointed to a divine governor of the world. By emphasizing ethics and the moral law as also the common element of all religion, the moral philosophers represented a secularizing and moralizing of the religious impulses—an influence that was becoming increasingly pronounced.[2]

This high and prestigious status of moral philosophy, however, did not endure. By the 1880s, the American college and university were experiencing those important shifts that led to our present institutions. For one thing, the sciences, especially the social sciences, broke away from moral philosophy to become specialized disciplines. For another, the commitment to a unified curriculum gave way to early undergraduate specialization, the proliferation of vocationalism and professional and graduate education, and an increasing emphasis on research, particularly scientific and social science research. By the late nineteenth and early twentieth centuries, moral philosophy had itself undergone some significant changes which, taken together with other alterations in the university, cast it also in an increasingly specialized role.

Santayana, Royce, and William James conceived philosophy and ethics very broadly, and they wrote as much for a general public as they did for their professional colleagues; that was the ideal of major philosophers in the late nineteenth century. That ideal did not endure. The rise of positivism led many philosophers to proclaim that moral statements and moral judgments had no roots in nature or reality at all, but were either emotive in origin or reflected merely personal subjective preferences. Only scientific statements had rational standing.[3]

A parallel stream, stimulated initially by the work of G. E. Moore and his enormously influential book, *Principia Ethica,* led in the direction of metaethics, that is, to an emphasis on theoretical questions about ethics: the grounds and justifications of moral statements, and on questions of the definition and status of ethical terms. Normative ethics, with its emphasis on the making of moral judgments, was rapidly put in the shade. Even when normative ethical theories were discussed, they tended to be discussed for their claims about certain metaethical concerns. The emphasis on metaethics came to constitute the mainstream of English language ethics well into the 1960s.[4] Rather than being thought of as "soft," philosophy—as if to ape science—became one of the "hardest" and most specialized disciplines, at least at the more prestigious institutions.

To be sure, the impact of continental existentialism and phenomenology began to make themselves felt during the thirties and forties, but they never achieved the prominence or centrality that was attained by metaethics and positivism. Sartre, Heidegger, and Jaspers were more objects of curiosity than influential figures. While the situation was different within departments of religion, where normative ethics remained comparatively strong, even religious ethics gradually came to be seen as a fairly specialized discipline, increasingly taught only within departments of religion and heavily oriented toward those majoring in religion or religious studies. By the 1950s and '60s, the most prominent textbooks and anthologies in moral philosophy were dominated by theoretical questions, with comparatively little attention being given either to normative ethics or to practical problems of applied or professional ethics.

A real shift became apparent only toward the end of the sixties. One important reason for the change was the severe criticism by a large number of philosophers themselves of logical positivism, criticism severe enough to displace it as a dominant philosophical movement.[5] Americans also began to appreciate anew the pragmatism of Charles Peirce, William James, and John Dewey. The displacement of positivism was also aided by new attitudes toward Marxism and existentialism; the earlier contempt that had been expressed by positivists for what they considered the unclear claims and language of those two movements gradually shifted toward a willingness to examine critically, but also sympathetically, these positions.

In addition to internal souces of change there were external causes. The social turmoil of the sixties and early seventies— struggles over civil rights, the Vietnam War, Watergate—led many to believe that moral problems and their resolution were important. Faculty members who had strong moral views began to express them more frequently, encouraged by students, and, in turn, encouraging them to do the same. By the mid-seventies, normative ethics was once again considered respectable—marked, for instance, by the acclaim that greeted John Rawls's book on justice. Courses in applied and professional ethics began to proliferate rapidly, not only in departments of philosophy and religion, but in many other university departments as well.

B. Current State of Ethics Teaching*

1. Methods of research

An important part of the work in The Hasting Center's Teaching of Ethics project has been the collection of information about present ethics teaching patterns at the college and professional school levels. There is an enormous amount of ethical instruction activity at present. Indeed, the number of persons and schools involved in ethics education is so large and growing so rapidly that any description of activities and programs will of necessity be incomplete and slightly out of date.

Because of the difficult task of describing the broad range of activity that currently exists in the teaching of ethics, our research group seized upon a number of strategies for sampling the available data. First, we solicited information through advertisements in various scholarly journals and newsletters. We were thus enabled to develop a sample of approximately fifteen hundred persons actively engaged in ethics instruction at higher education institutions. Second, we surveyed American college catalogues to determine the number, distribution, and variety of ethics courses currently being taught (1978). Third, we mailed a questionnaire to a random sample of 10 percent of the law professors listed in the *ABA Guide to Legal Education* who gave their area of teaching expertise as professional responsibility or legal ethics. Fourth, we established contacts with a number of academic professional societies such as the American Association for the Advancement of the Sciences, the American Council of

*The material in this section is adapted from: *The Teaching of Ethics in Higher Education: A Report by The Hastings Center* (Hastings-on-Hudson, N.Y.: The Hastings Center, 1980).

Learned Societies, the American Philosophical Association, the Modern Language Association, the American Association for the Advancement of the Humanities, the American Bar Association and the American Historical Association to ascertain the extent of ethics teaching activity among their members. Fifth, we drew upon our own previous ethics course in the areas of medicine, philosophy, and allied health. Sixth, we conducted site visits to a number of schools, including the University of Florida, Pace University Law School, Marist College, Fordham University, Vassar College, the United States Military Academy, and Siena Heights College. Seventh, we received visitors at The Hastings Center from a wide variety of schools, including Drexel University, New York University, Eastern Mennonite College, William Paterson College, the U.S. Army War College, the University of Illinois, Ohio State University, and St. Louis University, who gave us information about ethics teaching at their institutions. Eighth, we held a number of meetings at which experts in fields such as law, journalism, business, engineering, public policy, medicine, science, theology, and philosophy presented information about both their own teaching activities as well as activities in their disciplines and professions. Ninth, we commissioned a set of monographs on the teaching of ethics in medicine, law, business, journalism, public policy, engineering, and social science. These reports contain a great amount of empirical information on the nature and scope of ethical instruction in those areas. Finally, we collected a large amount of previously published material on the teaching of ethics which surveyed various fields, for example, the Society for Health and Human Values studies of medical ethics[6] and the Ethics and Values in Science and Technology Resource Directory[7] surveys of undergraduate and graduate programs in the areas of bioethics, professional ethics, and science and human values.

One might think that such a varied data base would give a complete and comprehensive guide to ethics teaching in higher education in America. But this is simply not the case. The number of schools, programs, professions and persons teaching in the broad area of ethics is so large that our data-gathering efforts have only skimmed the surface of this vast pool of information. Indeed, the absence of hard, empirical information on the "whos," "whys," and "wheres" of ethics teaching is surprising given the importance of the topic and the educational policy issues that are contingent upon having such information.

Finally, much of the data we have collected concerning the teaching of ethics has come to us from faculty actively engaged in the teaching of ethics. The dangers of bias in this sort of self-reporting are patent. We have tried to mitigate the exaggerations or distortions that can occur in the description of teaching activities by means of personal interviews, site visits, and crosschecks with experts in the relevant academic and professional fields. However, the large number of persons, courses, and schools involved has made it impossible to do this for each source. Undoubtedly errors of distortion and interpretation still remain in the observations presented in this report. Nonetheless, it seems worthwhile to present the data we have. It is to be hoped that this initial survey of the state of ethics teaching in America will prove to be a stimulus to further empirical inquiry concerning this important subject.

2. Results of catalogue survey

Many argue that during the past decade ethics studies have experienced a resurgence, not only within philosophy and theology, but also within many other departments and schools. If this is so, it is a phenomenon that has occurred with unusual speed given the inertia characteristic of most universities. A rough profile of ethics teaching in higher education institutions was obtained by a catalogue survey. An examination of 623 of the 2,270 1977–78 school catalogues revealed 2,757 ethics courses. We found that a resurgence, if any, in ethical instruction is not described in any detail or precision in catalogues.

We counted as an ethics course any one with a term such as "ethics," "values," "moral," or "responsibility," significantly occurring in the title, or any course whose description indicated a primary focus on ethics (e.g., "business and society," "journalism in a free society," "British intuitionists"). When in doubt we included borderline cases.

This catalogue survey turned up some surprising information. Eighty-nine of the colleges surveyed had no ethics courses listed. One medium-sized university, whose catalogue claimes its final objective for students is a "recognition of ethical ideals and the moral strength to put such ideas into daily living," listed only one undergraduate ethics course in the philosophy department. A common pattern in many colleges is a single course on ethics offered in the philosophy department with an additional course being given in a department of religion or theology, where schools have such departments.

Approximately one-fifth of the ethics courses were in professional ethics, two-fifths were courses in general theoretical ethics, and the remainder had ethics in some form as an important subtheme.

An interesting pattern emerged in the number of courses in "applied ethics." These are courses with distinctive and specific areas of concern such as bioethics, business ethics, the morality of war, or ethics and experimentation. Such courses concentrate on the application of moral theory to particular domains or problems rather than on the history or rationale of morality and ethics per se. The number of "applied ethics" courses was surprisingly large—50 percent of the ethics courses identified. However, the ratio of applied ethics courses to traditional ethics courses varied considerably among institutions. In general, large, prestigious universities offered more traditional theoretical ethics courses than did smaller, less well-known schools. In many schools the applied ethics courses were concentrated in science departments or professional schools, leaving the more theoretical courses to philosophy or theology departments. Applied ethics course topics ranged from "secretarial ethics" and "Christian business ethics" to "contemporary newspaper practices" and "pharmacy ethics."

The best-represented professions at both the graduate and undergraduate level in applied ethics are medicine, business, and law; and many of the universities surveyed offer a course in "bioethics" or "ethics and the life sciences." Approximately one-quarter of the surveyed ethics courses are taught in a philosophy department, while one-seventh of the total number of courses are taught by theology or religious studies departments; the rest are scattered among almost every other department.

A comparative sampling of ethics offerings in philosophy departments from the period 1950–65 revealed very few courses in "applied ethics." Moreover, a sample of thirty of the ethics textbooks and readers used during that period confirmed this impression since most focused almost exclusively on theoretical questions of ethics. Within the past decade ethics texts have increasingly emphasized very concrete and quite specific issues in ethics: abortion, truth-telling, confidentiality, justice, war and peace, sexual ethics, and the like. No less noteworthy has been the rapid proliferation of courses outside traditional philosophy and religious studies departments, almost all of them with an applied focus. Even in philosophy and religious studies departments significant content changes have recently occurred.

One of the most striking findings of the catalogue survey was the wide variation in the number of courses offered at different universities within a state, and in the number of courses offered in universities in different states. Arkansas, for example, has 20 colleges and universities; among them 28 ethics courses were offered during the 1977–78 period. In Kansas, by contrast, 23 colleges and universities offered 105 ethics courses during that period. At some colleges of comparable size, nearly two or three times as many courses in ethics were offered as in others. We found no systematic pattern in these variations and have no explanation for these differences. Our rough estimate is that 10–12,000 courses in ethics are offered in American undergraduate colleges.

3. The teaching of ethics at the undergraduate level

While we make no claim whatever to scientific completeness, the meetings we held, the correspondence we received, the surveys we conducted, the visits we made, and the consultations we carried out, allowed us to come to some tentative general conclusions. To remind you of one: in traditional departments of philosophy and religion, applied ethics courses are much more common now than a decade ago, and seem to be increasing with great rapidity. Another finding is the growth of ethics courses taught either outside traditional departments altogether or jointly sponsored by different departments.

We conclude that ethics is now receiving more systematic curricular attention than ten or twenty years ago. On the whole, student enrollments in ethics courses are growing; especially in ethics courses that are not taught in the traditional areas of philosophy or religion. But even the more traditional sorts of theoretically oriented or historical survey courses seem to be attracting more students than were enrolled five or ten years ago. Interestingly, while the number of students majoring in philosophy or religion appears to have declined in recent years, the number of students who have selected ethics courses may actually have increased. Since many ethics courses fall outside traditional humanities departments it may be useful to summarize some of our findings and impressions.

- Most new courses on ethics stress applied rather than theoretical concerns.
- Most new courses and programs are financed by "soft" rather than "hard" money.
- Most applied ethics courses or programs are less than ten years old.
- Most new courses are interdisciplinary in content (medical ethics, environmental ethics, social science ethics, etc.). New ethics courses are more likely to be team-taught than are traditional courses.
- The majority of new courses at the undergraduate level appear to be located in science departments or in preprofessional programs.
- Most ethics and values courses are elective rather than required.
- Many newer courses in ethics tend to use novel pedagogical techniques such as case studies, films, video tapes, panel discussions, visiting lecturers, class projects, etc.
- Most new ethics courses are oriented around specific ethical issues, e.g., euthanasia, bribery, atomic power, whistle-blowing, rather than being oriented around broad ethical themes, e.g., justice, individualism, deontology.
- A concern for ethics has manifested itself in the focus of required general education, humanities, or contemporary civilization courses.
- The impetus for establishing new or applied ethics courses and programs comes from many sources including faculty, students, and concerned administrators.
- It is most unusual for a student to major in ethics.

- There is no uniformity of goal or pedagogical method in teaching ethics to undergraduates.
- Most ethics courses are taught in classes of thirty or less.
- Comparatively, more ethics courses and programs have been instituted at schools that now have or had religious or denominational ties than at public institutions.
- Small liberal arts colleges tend to give more attention to ethical concerns in courses than do large state schools.
- A significant number of courses and programs exist in which ethics teaching has been linked to or inspired by social science work on moral development.
- New course offerings in philosophical or theological ethics tend to give greater emphasis to applied or practical issues.
- A large body of literature on applied ethics has appeared in the past ten years. Course bibliographies in ethics courses tend to draw liberally from this literature.

It may also be useful to mention some worries, disagreements, or frictions concerning ethics teaching at the undergraduate level. Some key points of concern among teachers, administrators, and students are:

- the kind of background and qualifications necessary for teaching ethics;
- disputes about the proper location for ethics courses within the curriculum;
- the absence of "hard" financing and real concern about enrollments for new courses and programs;
- disputes about the content appropriate to an undergraduate ethics course (these involve disagreements over the goals, methods, and content of such courses);
- worries about the possibility of indoctrination occurring in the ethics classroom;
- concern over the best or appropriate modes of evaluating undergraduate ethics teaching;
- the worry that the current rebirth of interest in ethics may be more of a fad than a real shift in educational policy;
- worries about taking time from other areas in the curriculum to give to ethics;
- disputes about whether ethics should be taught as a part of other courses or as a course in its own right;

- disputes about how ethics teaching should be defined and over what actually counts as ethics.

One of the most surprising findings is the degree to which persons involved in ethics teaching feel somewhat isolated from colleagues and peers. No real mechanisms, aside from professional society meetings in the humanities, exist for exchanging information and ideas about matters of pedagogy and methodology in this area. Many teachers of applied ethics courses are deeply concerned about their lack of experience in teaching such courses.

Many persons are worried about their ability to teach ethics effectively solely through the medium of courses or programs. Many instructors note that ethics education occurs in the family, the church, or in the dormitory and they feel frustrated at the expectation that a course on ethics will promote or guarantee personal virtue or desirable behavior. On the other hand, some educators worry that ethics education will become subservient to political, theological, or ideological aims of instructors. Most educators feel torn between the conflicting demands to effect behavioral change in students, and at the same time to teach without indoctrination or premature bias against alternative moral points of view. Students sometimes feel uncertain about the goals of ethics teaching and about the standards of assessment that will be used in evaluating their performance in the classroom.

It is difficult to assess the impact of ethics courses on students or the reception of new courses among faculty and administrators. This is owing to a number of factors: the ambiguity as to which courses count as ethics courses; the fact that more novel or new pedagogical techniques are utilized in ethics courses than are tried elsewhere in the curriculum; disagreements as to the proper aims and goals of ethics teaching; the fact that a student does not come *tabula rasa* to an ethics course; and because there is no agreement concerning the proper criteria for evaluation in ethics.

Despite these difficulties, it does seem safe to say that there has been a resurgence of interest in the teaching of ethics at the college level. This resurgence is characterized by the new and powerful impact of "applied" or "professional" ethics courses at the undergraduate level. It remains to be seen whether this new emphasis on applied ethics will continue. The precarious financial situation of many institutions may imperil the newer and less secure parts of the undergraduate curriculum, just as it has led on occasion to including ethics courses in an attempt to attract students.

C. Current Perceptions of Ethics Courses

1. Theoretical versus applied ethics

An interesting distinction in contemporary ethics teaching is between "applied" ethics and theoretical ethics. Those teaching applied ethics tend to focus their courses on particular problems or issues in science, technology, private or professional life. These courses focus on the analysis and solution of problems in real world contexts. Examples of such courses are medical ethics, environmental ethics, animal rights, the morality of war, or business and society.

One way to define applied ethics topics is to contrast them with the topics covered in traditional ethics courses. The latter courses focus either on historical treatments of great figures in ethics or upon key substantive themes of ethical theory. Thus, issues as utilitarianism, deontology, autonomy, and rights provide the focus for the traditional ethics course.

Practitioners of both types of courses disagree as to which is best suited for undergraduates. Many maintain that without firm roots in ethical theory, courses on applied ethics are misguided at best.[8] Many teachers of applied ethics claim that students are not sufficiently interested in ethical theory to study the principles of ethics for an entire term without getting down to cases. It is interesting to note that the dialectic between these two extremes has resulted in a certain amount of modification of views on both sides. This is best seen in the changes in books available for teaching both kinds of courses. Most contemporary anthologies and textbooks on ethics provide selections or chapters on what might be broadly termed "applied" subjects.[9] In textbooks and anthologies in such avowedly applied fields as bioethics, we note a trend to include chapters and selections on ethical theory.[10] The issue between the two schools now seems to be how much theory and how much application to include rather than whether pure theory or pure application is the correct approach.

2. Professional ethics versus liberal arts

Another major division in undergraduate ethics is between those in pre- and professional schools and those in the liberal arts. In many universities, students who have opted for professional careers (e.g., business and engineering) are in a preprofessional program emphasizing those subjects, and take highly specialized courses in the ethical issues of a profession. This may involve examination of specific ethical and valuational dilemmas faced by practicing professionals in a given field or a study of professional codes in a given field. Frequently, students examine case studies of professional dilemmas and are asked to reflect in a systematic fashion upon the various proposed solutions or resolutions of these moral problems.

In contrast to this emphasis on actual ethical dilemmas professionals will face is an emphasis on general ethics teaching as a perceived antidote to the kinds of socialization processes and pressures that all too frequently occur after one has selected a particular field of employment. The ethics course is seen as a prophylactic against the socializing tendencies of professions such as medicine or law, and so enables the student to be more humane and reflective in spite of the pressures of professional activities and careers. Often, the ethics course is one of the few places in which there is an opportunity to reflect on the role of professionals in society or about the history and aims of a profession. The conflicts between these different views of ethics teaching become patent when individuals introduce ethics courses into nontraditional, nonhumanities settings. Frequently, teachers in the social sciences or in courses on journalism, business, or nursing see no point in exposing their students to a liberal arts type of ethics course. Rather, after a minimal amount of ethical theory they spend most of the course on an examination of the professional quandaries and dilemmas in their profession.

3. Normative ethics versus metaethics

Another source of conflict among teachers of ethics is the differing emphases placed on normative ethical theories in contrast to metaethical concerns. For many years ethics courses in philosophy departments concentrated almost exclusively upon metaethical concerns—questions *about* ethics. Such questions included: could ethics be objective, did relativism prevail in ethical theorizing, what kinds of arguments could be adduced for holding a particular moral point of view, and why should one be ethical or moral at all? In the past decade a good deal of emphasis has been placed in ethics courses on studying and attending to problems of normative ethics, questions of what we ought to do and how we find out, rather than questions about metaethics. This has resulted in more attention to substantive normative issues such as whether civil disobedience can be justified, whether violence against the state is ever legitimate, and when it is appropriate to act paternalistically toward another person. The tension between the emphasis placed by some on metaethical questions and others on normative questions is very real. Some philosophers believe ethics courses have gone too far in the direction of dealing with normative issues, and have consequently left students helpless in dealing with the fundamental questions of how ethics is possible and plausible in the first place.[11] Many other teachers believe either (a) the distinction between normative and metaethics is spurious anyway, or (b) that issues of metaethics are primarily of concern to philosophers and are best not presented to undergraduate students. Only specialists, on this view, need deal with the problems of metaethical inquiry. While there has been some attempt in many recent ethics texts to accommodate questions of metaethics, it seems fair to say that many persons who teach ethics in philosophy and theology feel that the subject of metaethics is simply being neglected in the haste to make ethics courses palatable and relevant.

4. Philosophical versus religious ethics

Ethics scholars frequently argue about whether ethics ultimately needs to be rooted in some sort of theological or religious belief, or whether it is possible to build and teach a system of normative ethics solely on the basis of human reason and evidence. Many students come to an ethics course with a variety of church teachings on ethical matters. Some teachers make an effort to accommodate religious views about ethics in their courses. Other instructors see ethics courses as an opportunity to instill habits of critical thought about accepted views. There is disagreement among ethics teachers as to whether the undergraduate years are the most appropriate time for students to reflect critically upon their ethical beliefs. Some claim the undergraduate years are a time during which students should become even more firmly rooted in the actual traditions and principles that gird many theological views about ethics. While in most public institutions the secular-critical conception of ethics seem to prevail, the theological perspective has not completely disappeared from the teaching scene. There are a number of private schools and seminaries at which an ethics course involves the presentation of traditional theological beliefs and doctrines.

5. Moralizing versus philosophizing

Some tension presently exists between those who think that an ethics course should be the place where prescriptive views about morality are imparted to students and those who feel that prescription and moralizing have no place within ethics teaching. In many applied and theoretical ethics courses in a variety of institutional settings, teachers feel it appropriate to urge students to adopt certain forms of behavior, certain attitudes, or to accept specific beliefs about ethical and valuational matters. Frequently, an ethics course is used as a vehicle to expose students to certain counseling or therapeutic skills that involve making prescriptions. Many ethics teachers, however, believe this sort of moralizing or prescription has no place whatsoever in an ethics course. They believe that an ethics course should afford students an opportunity to make choices about what will or will not be believed. The use of the authority and power of the instructor to support moralizing is thought to be unfair, for students in such a situation often feel vulnerable, powerless, or helpless when faced with a moral message that they disagree with.

6. Ethics versus values

One of the most interesting of all the distinctions in ethics is reflected in the use of the terms "ethics" and "values." Those who teach courses with "ethics" in the title usually are committed to doing their teaching in a familiar traditional manner. Such courses generally involve some exposure to ethical theory and instruction on how principles and norms are applied to solve moral problems. The primary aim of the ethics course is to provide students with the theoretical apparatus needed to make moral judgments and select moral courses of conduct.

Those who use the term "values" to describe their teaching efforts usually do not agree with these goals. For example, many faculty in literature and history involved in the teaching of values courses understand their task to be to expose students to the fact that a normative, valuational, and subjective side of human life exists. Their task is conceived as more akin to moral phenomenology than to moral philosophy or analysis. Yet others understand the term "values" to signify courses that deal with the problems in professional ethics or applied ethics, in contradistinction to courses in normative ethics or ethical theory.

Still others use the term "values" to signify the fact that their teaching is inspired by a particular view of moral development or moral psychology. Finally, there are a number of individuals who use the term "values" to indicate that there are dimensions of valuation in addition to that of morality. Such persons believe that political, economic, social, and ideological values are as important, if not more important, to the understanding of moral issues than the pronouncements of moral philosophers.

The differences in language are instructive here because they indicate that many persons involved in the teaching of ethics courses have drastically different conceptions of what should be taught to undergraduate students. The sociology of the language used to describe ethics teaching is indicative of the many forces at work in shaping the content and direction of the undergraduate college curriculum.

As philosophers we think, naturally enough, that the meanings of the terms "ethics" and "values" should be fixed so that they are used unequivocally in every occurrence. Alas, we have no power to fix the meanings, though we hope this public statement of the variety of uses will sensitize ethics teachers to the need to make clear in their course descriptions, exactly what they will do.

II. Methodological and Substantive Issues in the Teaching of Undergraduate Ethics

A. Goals in the Teaching of Undergraduate Ethics*

Considerable confusion results from disagreement about the purpose of ethics courses. Should such courses promote virtue? Should the goal be to change behavior? Should they seek only to teach rational thinking? Or should all of these purposes, perhaps, be sought? In addition to the problem of desirable goals, there is the question of what goals can be reached given a variety of student backgrounds, capacities, desires, and expectations.

Most teachers of a first course in ethics want students to read the work of at least some of the important figures in the history of ethics. John Stuart Mill is an author almost everyone would agree is one of those figures, an author who is widely admitted by academics to be a writer of clear prose, a writer who produced his works, not for academics, but for all educated people. Students, however, often find Mill difficult to read. They complain that the sentences are too long, and often they simply get lost in his arguments. If large numbers of students have trouble with Mill, that trouble is nothing compared with the difficulty they have with Aquinas, Kant, or Aristotle. This is not to claim that most students cannot read these

*The material in this section is adapted from: *The Teaching of Ethics in Higher Education: A Report by The Hastings Center* (Hastings-on-Hudson, N.Y.: The Hastings Center, 1980).

authors with understanding. There are so many who cannot, however, that a very serious problem is posed for the teacher in the selection of course material, and therefore in the direction a course can take.

Thus, when teachers try to determine the appropriate goals for a course in ethics, they must keep squarely in mind the educational situation and background of their students. The Report of The Hastings Center Project on the Teaching of Ethics proposes five goals for ethics courses, and they can be summarized briefly here.[12]

The first is that of "Stimulating the Moral Imagination." That is, an attempt to engage the emotions and feelings of students, to lead them to see that human beings live their lives in a web of moral relationships, to recognize that a consequence of moral positions and rules can be actual suffering or happiness, and to accept the fact that moral conflicts are often inevitable and difficult. The emotional side of students must be elicited or evoked—empathy, feeling, caring, sensibility. Morality matters; it is at the core of human lives.

A second goal is that of "Recognizing Ethical Issues." A very fine line separates stimulation of the moral imagination and a recognition of ethical issues. It is precisely at the point when the imagination has been stimulated that the classroom emphasis should shift from the emotions and feelings that have been evoked to a conscious, rational attempt to identify those elements that represent appraisal and judgment. What evidence does empathy provide for moral judgments? How do we recognize a moral issue in the first place? What are the differences among political, economic, and moral problems?

A third goal is that of "Developing Anaytical Skills." In order to recognize moral issues, we need to examine concepts such as "justice," "autonomy," "dignity," "rights"; prescriptive moral statements; and ethical principles and moral rules. This analysis provides us with a crucial means by which some order is given to the relatively untutored deliverances of experience and previous conditioning. An important part of any course in ethics should be assisting students to develop those skills—by a careful dissection of arguments, by an attempt to understand both the logical and social implications of our moral stands, by attempts to understand the importance of coherence and consistency.

The fourth goal is that of "Eliciting a Sense of Moral Obligation and Personal Responsibility." "Why ought I to be moral?"—that is a fundamental question in ethics, and a topic to which students should rapidly be introduced. Yet even if that question can be answered in a preliminary fashion, other difficult issues remain. Am I obliged to act on my moral conclusions, or is there a gap between theory and action? Does my freedom as a moral agent require that I take moral responsibility for what I do? Any course on ethics must explore the role, in practice, of freedom and personal responsibility. It makes no sense to talk of ethics unless one presupposes that individuals have some freedom to make moral choices and that they are responsible for the choices they make.

The fifth goal is "Tolerating—and Resisting—Disagreement and Ambiguity." Students need to learn to tolerate the disagreements and be prepared to accept the inevitable ambiguities in attempting to examine and solve ethical problems. We can and do differ with our closest friends on matters of ethics, and many ethical issues admit of no final, clear resolution. Nonetheless, while there must be toleration of disagreement and ambiguity, there must no less be an attempt to locate and clarify the sources of disagreement, to resolve ambiguity as far as possible, and to see if ways can be found to overcome differences of moral viewpoint and theory. Civility can make a significant difference when people differ with each other, and it can help them better to work together on hard dilemmas.

In addition to these general goals, of course, there will be different pertinent topics for different parts of a course in ethics, or different kinds of courses in ethics. Courses in professional ethics often will introduce students to various professional codes, to the mores and values of particular professions, and to the historical and cultural background of those professions. Courses in applied ethics would naturally gravitate toward such concrete issues as abortion, civil rights, war and peace, whistle-blowing, and so on. Courses in ethical theory would explore in depth such topics as utilitarianism, natural law, and deontology.

For many, however, the goal outlined above will not be sufficient. Many believe that courses in ethics should directly seek to change student behavior.[13] After all, is not ethics all about how people ought to behave? We share with the authors of The

Hastings Center Report the belief that the changing of behavior ought not to be an *explicit* goal of a course in ethics. For one thing, it would be exceedingly naive to expect much improvement of any kind from a single course on ethics. Students are exposed to a wide variety of influences outside of any one course. For another, in order to bring about direct immediate changes in student behavior, professors might well be tempted to pursue highly dubious techniques of manipulation and coercion; at the least, the temptation to crudely indoctrinate would be very strong. Moreover, an explicit attempt to change student behavior would beg many important moral questions, precisely those questions that ought to be pursued in an ethics course: Just what constitutes good or correct behavior? What virtues are appropriate for human beings? What behavior is right when two or more valid moral principles are in conflict?

Yet if, for a variety of reasons, an explicit attempt to change behavior is an inappropriate goal, this is hardly to deny that students ought to be led to see the importance of taking moral responsibility for their actions. If a student's careful analysis of a moral issue leads that student quite freely to recognize the need for a change of behavior, then one would hope a course would set the groundwork for such a change. The question is not whether courses should seek to change behavior, but whether the course would help a student to know the importance of changing his or her behavior if that was what a moral judgment seemed to entail.

The question of the relationship between courses in ethics and the future character and behavior of students will continue to be a vexing one. "Can virtue be taught?" was a question raised 2,500 years ago by Socrates, and it is a question that has continued to intrigue educators and teachers ever since. The rapidly developing field of moral psychology may help to provide some help in answering the question, and those teaching ethics at the undergraduate level should at the very least familiarize themselves with that literature. While the results of research in that field are too preliminary to date to provide any very explicit guidance to teachers of ethics at the college level, much of the research is very suggestive and can help to provide teachers with a greater insight into the psychological situation of the students they teach.

B. Indoctrination and Indispensability

Indoctrination is a topic closely related to the question of goals. Frequently, a concern about the goals of ethics teaching really cloaks a deeper worry about the content of ethics courses and the means by which such material is presented to students. Others worry that, in a pluralistic society such as ours, the study required to understand some one moral philosophy or set of moral tenets will not occur, with the result that students will not learn any morality from their ethics instruction.

Often, those who reject the view that all moral claims are equally correct also reject the view that all moral claims have an equal right to be heard. They argue that moral issues and normative ethical theories are too important to leave to chance or to the ability of students to reason, so we must ensure that our students (as well as all citizens) hold the "proper" moral views.

Without attempting to offer a definition, we can say that indoctrination occurs when someone tries to inculcate a view without the intended learner exercising his or her own reasoning ability. The opposite of that is captured by several of the goals in the teaching of ethics that were mentioned above, such as stimulating the moral imagination, developing analytical skills, and tolerating and enjoying disagreement.

Dispensability aims at students being able to reason and reach decisions about moral problems and normative ethical theories without the aid of the teacher. The teacher is needed, of course, to stimulate the student, to impart the basic skills, to correct obvious errors in reasoning, and to show that options are available from great thinkers and traditions. Teachers of ethics must walk a fine line between the desire to ensure that students become morally sensitive, contributing members of our society and what we consider the highest obligation of teaching, viz., to make oneself dispensable as a result of teaching.

It is easy to point out, once the distinctions have been drawn, that our aim is dispensability, not indoctrination. We can resist the conclusion that indoctrination is an inevitable goal in the teaching of ethics and can reject the claim that all views are equally correct. We think that some views, both specific moral stands and normative ethical theories, are correct, and yet we think that the competing views should be heard. Our suggestion is that we better understand this when we understand that indoctrination is undesirable and dispensability is desirable.

C. Qualifications for the Teaching of Undergraduate Ethics*

The recent rapid proliferation of courses in ethics, particularly in applied and professional ethics, has made pressing the question of appropriate qualifications for ethics teachers. Few doubt the necessity of an advanced degree in philosophy or religion to teach a course specifically on traditional philosophical or religious ethics, but the situation is far less clear for courses taught outside traditional departments. While the renewed interest in ethics has drawn heavily on those with specific training in that field, it has also attracted some who have no special professional qualifications at all. The concern to have qualified ethics teachers has led to an examination of ethics teaching qualifications. Can someone trained in ethics teach bioethics without a background in biology and medicine? A trained moral philosopher may have superb skills in dealing with ethical theory, but have neither the professional nor personal background necessary, say, to teach a course that focuses on ethical problems in the practice of journalism. Yet those who have an appropriate background in a particular professional field, in turn, may have no special qualifications to deal systematically with the ethical problems of those fields.

What are adequate qualifications? With the exception of courses specifically in religion and philosophy departments, we do not think it is necessary that teachers of applied and professional ethics have an advanced degree in moral philosophy or moral theology. We believe that those teachers ought, however, to have a very solid grounding in their professional field and *also* have some adequate grounding in ethics. But what is such a solid grounding? What additional academic or professional grounding ought a person to have beyond the professional training already received in his or her own field? It should at least require a broad

*The material reported in this section is adapted from: *The Teaching of Ethics in Higher Education: A Report by The Hastings Center* (Hastings-on-Hudson, N.Y.: The Hastings Center, 1980).

familiarity with the language, concepts, and characteristic modes of analysis of the other discipline—what that discipline considers to be an appropriate way of handling issues that arise in its field, how it makes use of evidence or data and evaluates them, and how it distinguishes between good work and bad. The consensus Report of The Hastings Center Project on the Teaching of Ethics proposes that at least one year of education in another field should be aimed for, whether gained in one bloc or cumulatively.[14] Some are undoubtedly able to educate themselves entirely; but most need to work, at least for a time, with those trained in the other field. In addition, practical experience with the kinds of problems that arise in a profession is needed to enable the teacher to understand sensitively the concrete dynamics that mark any wrestling with specific moral concerns.[15]

An attractive solution to the problem of qualifications is team-teaching. Here two or more teachers, each drawing upon the knowledge of his or her own discipline, work closely with someone trained in another discipline. At its very best, it not only enables students better to understand the modes of reasoning and analysis employed in different disciplines, but also provides them with a vivid example of people trained in different fields struggling together to work through moral problems. Of course team-teaching often encounters many practical problems. It is frequently expensive, and because of departmental structures in universities, very difficult to manage as a practical matter. One real hazard is that sometimes such courses provide no more than material presented by different disciplines in a parallel way, but with no meeting of the parallel approaches.

Two conditions seem necessary for good team-teaching. First, the courses should be structured so that the technical material from the non-ethics discipline is tightly integrated with the ethics material. Second, those engaged in team-teaching should be fully prepared to grapple with material from their colleague's discipline. The initial goal of team-teaching should be the mutual education of the instructors. If they cannot find ways of educating each other, it is hardly likely that their students will make the necessary connections. However, we also think that team-teaching should not become a substitute for the more important task of a teacher's developing a decent grounding in another field. Team-teaching can be part of that education, but given the difficulties of organizing and sustaining a permanent interdisciplinary course, most teachers of ethics will eventually be forced to teach alone.

D. The Good and the Teacher Who Is Good

The distinction between the morally wise person and the person knowledgeable about morality is easy to draw. The morally wise person is someone you would consult if you had a difficult moral problem: usually these persons are friends or perhaps physicians or ministers. Such persons, presumably, know something about normative ethics, but usually they are not formally trained in the subject. In contrast, someone might have extensive knowledge of normative ethical systems but be insensitive to the actual needs of people, or not be a very good person. Students, of course, learn by precept as well as concept, and although we might hope that the teacher of ethics could serve as a role model, we do not think we can count on it. Certainly the instructor should know that one way to teach ethics is through personal example, though as a teacher of ethics one would have to generalize from one's own case or abstract the general guidelines for the students. It is no exaggeration to say that moral lessons will be taught by the teacher of ethics, whether these lessons are intended or not, as a result of grading papers, responding to questions, handling difficult situations in class, and the like. Most (but not all) teachers of ethics recognize this and act accordingly.

Students also learn from institutional behavior. If tenured teachers are fired or competent Marxists not hired or women discriminated against, the institution is conveying moral lessons to the students. Moral lessons also are conveyed, not only by the school, but by family, friends, TV, and churches. This complicates the picture of what the teacher does, but it also dilutes the influence of that teacher.

Those who teach ethics are usually better able to justify or rationalize their actions than most, for their training and study has equipped them to marshall evidence. This means that the morally wise person trained in ethics is in a better position to do more good for more people, and the morally wicked person trained in ethics is in a position to do more harm.

E. Evaluation*

1. Is evaluation possible?

Everyone wants to get their money's worth, whether a student in a course or a dean considering the worth of a teacher or a program. To make such decisions, evaluations are needed. There are two different kinds of evaluation: an evaluation *within* (or *internal* to) a course as to whether the student has learned the material that is being taught and has acquired the skills that were to be imparted, and an evaluation *of* a course. An evaluation *of* a course is a determination of whether or not a course has succeeded in teaching the material and imparting the skills it advertises that it can, and also whether those materials and skills are worth having. It will be suggested below that the evaluation *within* an ethics course is on at least as good a footing as evaluation within other courses in the university. The evaluation *of* the ethics course is a bit more complicated, though one strong claim we make is that the student evaluation of such courses cannot legitimately be the only evaluation of the ethics course.

If the general goal of evaluation is to assess both the importance and the quality of the ethics courses, the following questions seem especially relevant to any decisions as to methodology: the first two questions concern evaluation *within* a course and the third the evaluation *of* the course.

1. Are there traditional modes of evaluation in the humanities appropriate for evaluating courses on ethics and values?
2. Is ethics as a subject matter unique or special in its internal evaluation difficulties?
3. Can objective evaluations *of* any course in the humanities be conducted?

For the impatient reader our answers are yes, no, and maybe. But the reasons for these answers need to be examined.

Most humanists agree there are standards for the evaluation of student course performance *within* ethics courses. Humanists do not differ from other scholars in their proclivity to judge student performance and assess student work. Anyone who takes a course in philosophy, theology, or literature becomes aware quickly that

*The material in this section is adapted from Arthur L. Caplan, "Evaluation and the Teaching of Ethics," in Daniel Callahan and Sissela Bok, eds., *Ethics Teaching in Higher Education* (New York: Plenum Press, 1980).

standards of competence and excellence do indeed exist in these fields. If anything, the tendency in ethics courses is probably to devote too much time to the evaluation of student performance. Classroom discussions, tests, and writing assignments provide students with ample opportunities to have their nascent analytical ethical skills and beliefs critically assessed by faculty. Classroom performance, quizzes or tests, and written papers are the traditional modes of evaluation in the humanities in general and, in particular, in courses on ethics and values. The real issue concerning evaluation of student performance is not whether modes of evaluation exist, but whether the traditional means of doing evaluations within the humanities will suffice for the evaluation of courses in ethics.

There is little reason to think that traditional modes of evaluation will not suffice in ethics courses. The easiest and most direct ways of determining a student's mastery of ethics are to observe the student in classroom discussion and to read examples of the student's written work. The ability to identify ethical issues, the skill with which ethical theory can be applied to analyze problems, the liveliness of the moral imagination—all can be ascertained by the instructor who carefully attends to what students say in class and on paper.

Although cynics may sneer and complain "Watch what students do, not what they say," the fact is that they must say "it" if there is to be any hope of them doing "it." Given the hard reality of this causal sequence, evaluation in the ethics course must focus around thought and not action.

Still, it might be argued that time and enrollments do not permit close faculty supervision of students. Nor will students from the sciences or business gladly suffer ethics courses that require term papers or erudite review essays. But neither of these worries impugn the validity of the traditional modes of student evaluation within humanities courses. The former may say something about the mechanics of successful teaching (small classes, much discussion time). The latter may say something about the kinds of topics and cases that must be used to rivet the less than enthusiastic student's attention. Still, a doggedly persistent critic of traditionalism in evaluation methodology might protest that all the talk of modes of evalution misses the point—neither students nor faculty know what counts as good or bad work in ethics.

Whether an instructor uses case studies, papers, classroom debates, or special videotapes, no one will know what makes for good work in matters ethical or valuational. Is objective evaluation in ethics possible? While modes of evaluation exist, the critic continues, taste, personal idiosyncracy, prejudice, and mood combine in one very fickle criterial jumble of evaluational assessment.

However, two points are particularly germane to respond to the concern about objective evaluation. First, the concern about objectivity, if only about evaluations within ethics, is really a disguised version of that favorite old chestnut of positivism—ethical emotivism. Without that assumption there is no reason to presume that objective judgments of students' ethical reasoning and skills are more problematic than in any other area. Since instructors do know and agree on what good arguments are, what legitimate value puzzles are, and what lively moral imaginations are (both personally and interpersonally), there is at least some reasons for thinking that ethics evaluation is less problematic. Secondly, objectivity becomes of particular concern when there is a reason to suspect partiality on the part of the evaluator. This is why, as was noted earlier, program evaluations by colleagues and peers are so suspect. But instructors are, happily, in a better position to assess their impact on students and vice versa. Consequently, quality assessment is feasible where mechanisms are used to ensure this much needed impartiality ("blind" grading of papers, steering away from articles written by the instructor, etc.). If impartiality can be secured, objectivity has a good chance of being secured as well.

A passionate argument in favor of an evaluation strategy that most people working in the field of ethics and values already believe in and use regularly may seem strange. But a defense of traditionalism concerning evaluation within ethics courses becomes understandable when juxtaposed against a description of some of the narrow modes of evaluation currently gaining some favor in certain academic circles.

2. Traditional sources of information

There are at least seven sources of information about the efficacy and utility of teaching ethics within a course or program,

many of them also being ways to make an evaluation *of* the
ethics course. Some are traditional techniques in the humanities,
others are newer and less well articulated. Both types may be
useful, and the inexperienced teacher of ethics may do well to
experiment.

(1) *Classroom Observation.* The performance of students and
teachers in classroom settings is important. Do students partici-
pate in discussions? Are the instructor's views questioned and
challenged? Do students incorporate course readings and lecture
material into their discussions? Do students seem eager and willing to engage in discussion and debate about substantive moral
issues?

(2) *Written Evidence.* Can students analyze moral problems in
a clear and cogent manner in written assignments? Does their
writing about ethical issues reflect increased sensitivity to course
content as the course progresses? Are the students able to con-
struct their own analyses and plausible solutions to moral problems? Are students able to go beyond the lectures and readings in
constructing their interpretations and solutions?

(3) *Interviews.* Can students, as shown in direct conversation
with instructors, integrate classroom material into their everyday
lives? Do students have opinions as to the quality and utility of
lectures and readings? Are they able to conduct a reasonably
coherent discussion about a moral problem or ethical issue of
public moment?

(4) *Games and Simulations.* Are students capable of analyzing
hypothetical or idealized moral problems? Can they "take sides"
in a debate and articulate the reasons (if any) underlying various
moral points of view? Can the student put himself or herself "in
another person's shoes" and see moral problems from another
perspective?

3. Nontraditional sources of information

(5) *Peer Interviews.* What do friends and associates of students
say about their attitudes, beliefs, and behavior relative to moral
matters subsequent to course or program instruction? Is student
sensitivity to the existence of moral issues increased? Do they
tend to articulate and defend moral points of view more readily

than prior to classroom instruction? Are they better able to aid their peers in analyzing moral problems?

(6) *Observation Outside the Classroom.* Do other teachers notice any shifts in the attitudes, beliefs, or arguments of students subsequent to or during the ethics course or program? Do students appropriately discuss moral issues and problems outside the ethics classroom?

(7) *Tests.* There are a number of tests presently available for measuring the level of moral reasoning of individuals. Many of these tests have not been applied at the college level. Nonetheless, a standardized test or scale, e.g., Rest's D.I.T.,[16] may provide evidence of cognitive or affective change as a consequence of ethical instruction. While there are numerous difficulties in interpreting the results of such tests, they may enable us to measure cognitive or affective change subsequent to classroom instruction.

No single mode is distinctively *the* best way of obtaining information about the teaching of ethics. Sometimes the effects of an ethics course are best seen in students who have left university life and are well along in their post-academic careers. Some of the most sensitive techniques for observing subtle changes in abilities, knowledge, skills, and behavior involve kinds of observation and interaction that are often difficult to achieve.

We claim there are many ways to evaluate performance within an ethics course, though one does have to make reference, for the most part, to the goals of teaching that ethics course. Implicit in the statement of the ways to evaluate are the goals. When we say that we want to determine if students can analyze moral issues and present arguments that are clear and cogent, we assume that being able to analyze and present arguments is a good thing. If we want to determine how well a course has succeeded in teaching students how to handle arguments on their own without the aid of the teacher, we assume dispensability is a good thing. We plead guilty to assuming the goals are good ones, for it is obvious that one cannot make an evaluation *of* a course simply by seeing if the goals that are set up within a course are met, for we have to know if the goals that are set up are *worth* reaching. We have presented considerations along the way for such tests, and we certainly assume that given some connection between moral beliefs and action, and some further connection between clear reasoning and justified beliefs, few will quarrel with the goals that we have set out and the others that we have implicitly assumed.

4. Criteria

There are many levels and settings for the teaching of ethics. It is, thus, patent that no one set of criteria can guide evaluation and assessment in this area. Moreover, since the criteria of evaluation must remain sensitive to the goals and purposes motivating ethical instruction—and these vary—there will be a corresponding variation in the types of criteria chosen by instructors, students, administrators, and peers. Nonetheless, it may be useful, especially to those not experienced in the teaching of ethics or teaching in the humanities, to have available an example of criteria used in many ethics classrooms. The criteria described below have proved useful in our teaching. While they are criteria to be used *within* an ethics course, we make an evaluation *of* the course by determining how effectively the goals and ends listed in the criteria are met.

(1) *Quality of Arguments for Moral Views.* There is a large difference between assessing the "correctness" of a given moral position and the quality of a moral argument. Sound positions in ethics ought to be supported by good reasons. Students should be sensitive to the difference between moral conclusions and the assumptions and premises of moral argument. Familiarity with a broad range of moral theories, and the ability to relate moral beliefs to these theories and their constitutive rules and principles, form the heart of competence in ethics. Students in any ethics course should be able to articulate, verbally and in written assignments, coherent moral arguments rooted in moral theory.

(2) *Mastery of Theories and Principles of Ethics.* As in any other discipline or field there is a body of theory and knowledge in ethics that students must master. The difficulty confronting the instructor is that there is usually much too much material available for a single course. Moreover, instructional competence will vary over the range of available material, and students must not be overwhelmed by a barrage of names, traditions, qualifications,

and schools of thought. Despite these difficulties, it seems reasonable to require that all students be able to demonstrate a high degree of familiarity with the range and scope of ethical traditions presented in the classroom and that the basic concepts and terms of ethics analysis and argument (i.e., utility, principle, duty, rights, etc.) introduced in discussions and readings be mastered.

(3) *Identification of Moral Issues.* Students should be able to identify various sorts of moral issues. The ability should extend beyond classroom examples and case studies to materials or discussions drawn from other disciplines, fields, and nonclassroom sources.

(4) *Ability to Appreciate Both Sides of a Position.* All students should be prepared to take moral views and defend them, not just for the sake of argument, though that is an important exercise, but to acquire the ability to "see the other side" of an argument and to empathize with the moral points of view of others. By the end of a course students should be willing and eager to engage in moral debate and theoretically inspired ethical argumentation.

It is, of course, possible to evaluate using many more criteria than these four discussed here. But these four seem minimally necessary to make an evaluation *of* ethics courses. When combined with the various modes of gathering information discussed earlier, they should provide a solid basis for evaluation both *within* a course and *of* it.

III. Problems of Pedagogy in the Teaching of Undergraduate Ethics

A. Moral Problems in the Classroom

John Dewey made some suggestions so sensible they were revolutionary:

> If we compare this condition with that of the well-ordered home, we find that the duties and responsibilities that the child has there to recognize do not belong to the family as a specialized and isolated institution, but flow from the very nature of the social life in which the family participates and to which it contributes. The child ought to have the same motives for right doing and to be judged by the same standards in the school, as the adult in the wider social circle to which he belongs. Interest in community welfare, an interest that is intellectual and practical, as well as emotional—an interest, that is to say, in perceiving whatever makes for social order and progress, and in carrying these principles into execution—is the moral habit to which all the special school habits must be related if they are to be animated by the breath of life.[17]

Perhaps it is easier to draw attention to the moral problems that arise in the classroom for younger students than for undergraduates but it is still possible. Here are some suggestions about problems that are common and a few that are not.

A typical moral problem, though it is not usually perceived that way by students, or even faculty, involves the student who wants to pursue a point in which only he or she is interested, or who does not see a criticism of his or her own view that others think is obvious. For example, suppose a student wants to defend psychological ego-

ism—the view that the only motive for voluntary action is self-bene-
fit—as a way to defend ethical egoism, the view that actions are
right as they tend to benefit self. Most students think both views are
"dumb," and want to do something else. The teacher now faces a
moral problem, for the student can be put off by saying the concerns
will be considered after class. However, the occasion can also be
used to show that sometimes we are justified in taking up an issue
because someone is deeply concerned about it. This is not to claim
that there are no problems so obscure that we are not justified in
saying that we will have to discuss them in private. It is to say that
teachers frequently face a choice which is not easy to make, and
which is, in part, moral. One cannot simply tell the other students
that it is their obligation to listen to their fellow student, though one
might try to awaken a sense of community by asking others to help
clarify the question or problem. This helps to dispel the brittle individualism and competition that sometimes infects classrooms. One
might talk about one's own fallibility in pursuing topics; ask
whether it is better to err on the side of supposing a question to be of
importance and general interest. One can let some answers to these
questions emerge, then show the inevitable ethical reasoning that is
involved and evaluate that reasoning as is done with the reasoning
of Mill and Kant.

Every class has tests, quizzes, examinations, papers, reports, or
some other method of evaluating student performance. These exercises raise many moral issues. Should there be grades at all? Many
students think there should not, and when pressed will invariably
present their reasons concerning obligation and value. They will say
that a university or college is better if there are no grades because. . . . No final evaluation of the reasons is needed to make this
a worthwhile exercise in applied ethics. One of the topics that must
come up, though, is the responsibility, usually a quasi-legal one, of
the instructor to turn in grades. Should, morally, the instructor risk
loss of job to uphold the value of a possible future university system? Should, morally, the students insist on this? What would Mill
say about this? Kant?

In most ethics course, some sort of group project can be assigned.
Usually the group presents a report to the rest of the class, an oral
report accompanied by an outline or paper. The outline or paper is
rewritten as a group paper that is then handed in to be graded along

with the other parts of students' course work. A problem posed for the students involves the grading of the group report: should each student in the group receive the overall grade given to the oral report and the written report? In every group some students contribute more: Is it fair or just that everyone receive the same grade? How can one determine who gets what grade? Should the fellow group members have a say? How much of a say? These questions, their clarification, and placement within the context of normative ethics make for an important part of the course. Not only do the questions concern moral issues, they show students that they are personally involved in moral problems. Once the involvement of all humans in this matter is established, it becomes easier to talk about moral issues and ethical dilemmas that others might face.

One reason ethics teachers might not pursue these questions is that, unlike purely theoretical problems, this set of problems requires an actual solution because the teacher does have to assign grades. It raises the moral problem for the teacher of ethics as to what is the appropriate means to settle that moral question. However difficult these moral problems are for the ethics teacher, it is our view that it is useful to let them arise in the classroom. Students will invariably suggest a vote to settle the issue, and faculty will have trouble with that because of their professional responsibility. This tension, too, is instructive. It shows the teacher as beset by moral problems just as the students are. (Once students realize that faculty members have moral problems they won't be as surprised when they see them drinking a beer at the local pub, or goofing off in their offices, or walking with their children in the park.)

Another topic that arises in class is student responsibility and attendance. Suppose a student exercises an option, given by the instructor, not to attend class (either a certain number of times per term, or whenever the student chooses) and thereby misses an assignment. Suppose the assignment is a group of readings plus a quiz, or a short paper, and the student comes into class unprepared to take the quiz. Should the teacher allow the student a makeup? Require the student to take the quiz right then? Require the student to take it and not count it? These questions and others should all be raised before the problem arises, not only for the instructive value of the problems, but also to protect the instructor.

These sorts of moral problems can profitably be discussed in ethics classes. Although useful in applied ethics courses, they are especially useful in a general ethics course because no pool of actual moral problems is brought in from an applied field, and because there is often a sense among students that they don't have moral problems.

It would be possible to teach a first course in normative ethics totally within the context of the actual moral problems that arise in the classroom by showing how the competing normative ethical theories apply to those problems. Alternatively, lectures on the major normative ethical theories could be illustrated with problems that lie solely outside the classroom. One teacher might proceed dialectically, from the responses of students to presentation of moral issues whether of the classroom or nonclassroom sort. Another teacher might cover only the great moral theories. Any format can meet the goals of an ethics course, i.e., students can learn how to recognize moral issues, become sensitive to them, learn how to examine them critically, etc. We are inclined to involve students as much as possible, because there is reason to accept John Dewey's suggestion that people learn best when they take an active part in the learning process. But this involvement or the use of give-and-take discussion (or any method) depends upon the personality of the teacher as well as the method itself.

B. Teaching Students how to Choose among Theories

Once students are concerned about a normative ethical theory (the most general method of reaching justified moral judgment) they are struck by the need to have some way of choosing among ethical theories. Much of what teachers do in general ethics classes is to demonstrate how to evaluate normative ethical theories. Consider utilitarianism as an illustration. While it may be true that egoism is the first theory that the largest group of students selects as its normative theory, after reflection, utilitarianism is frequently the first theory chosen. Most teachers of general ethics assign J. S. Mill, and others at least describe that position. Imagine the student who has chosen utilitarianism as his or her normative ethical theory. The student is aware, let us assume, that the theory functions to generate singular moral judgments, and has chosen utilitarianism, in part, because of its power to do that.

Two main criticisms are directed against most forms of utilitarianism: (1) there are a number of counterexamples involving other proposed sources of obligation, and (2) there is a problem of distributive justice.[18] If you promise your dying father to scatter his ashes in his homeland, but it would not maximize good to do so, then, on utilitarian grounds, you have no obligation to keep the promise. (Assume that no one else knows about it, that you won't have sleepless nights as a result of not keeping the promise, and so on.) A slave system in which one quarter of the population serves the rest might maximize good, although it is not just. This kind of problem is standard fare for ethics courses. The student realizes his or her chosen theory can be criticized. The student may respond to the criticisms, hold the theory in face of the criticisms, become discouraged about theories and adopt a nonrational theory about accepting normative theories, or hold a "best theory" view. The "best theory" approach consists of a comparison with other theories: if your theory does the best job it is acceptable—even though there are criticisms.

The ethics teacher has an intellectual obligation to guide the student in the next step. If the teacher says nothing, most students conclude that all the theories have equally serious criticisms and that theories are adopted according to one's inclinations. Some claim the justification is a species of choice ("existentialist leap") or that this shows the futility of philosophy. The latter view can be accompanied by an invitation to become a member of the Hare Krishna Society or some equally all-encompassing organization. Perhaps this is the way to go, but we doubt that very many would want to go that way.

What are the options? One can survey the main normative theories and then ask the students to choose among them. This is a good approach, although the teacher then has to return to the problem of choice when the survey is finished. One can offer a method of evaluating normative theories and then tell the students that you, as teacher, are their guide in the application of the criterion, but not their guru. Each teacher should probably say what his or her own view is, for otherwise students are upset by what they perceive as lack of commitment, but no one should preach one's own view as gospel. We all think the normative view we have adopted is correct, the best one, and all that, but what is important for our students is that they learn how to discover and defend their own view, not that they hold a view that happens to be the one true one. (We all know, of course, that our own view may very well turn out not to be the one true one anyway!)

The condition of being able to select the best normative ethical theory without its being selected for the student by the teacher is what we have called dispensability. The student does not, finally, need the teacher to choose the correct theory or, at the height of the art of teaching, even the method of choosing the correct theory.

In addition to criticisms directed to the theory a student holds, there is the inevitable disagreement among students about which normative ethical theory is correct. One student will be a Kantian, another an egoist, and a third a utilitarian. The teacher at this point *must* make a decision; this is one of those situations where not deciding to do something is actually to do something. Mere disagreement bogs down, almost always, because students lack a means for working it out. The teacher has to supply the means, and failure to supply it conveys, usually, the message that there is no framework, and that the selection of a normative theory is arbitrary or a matter of taste. The teacher may actually believe that he or she has at least an intellectual obligation to point out that Mill thought that everyone actually used the principle of utility, that Kant thought that everyone actually had the categorical imperative in mind when he or she formulated maxims, that Hobbes thought that individuals could not help but act to secure what they perceived as their own good, and so on. While one contemporary view holds the selection of a normative ethical theory to be a matter of noncognitive or nonrational choice, that is but one view.

Where there is criticism of the normative theory chosen, and where there is disagreement with other students about which normative ethical theory is correct, the discussion of the question is rooted in an interest in normative ethics.

A bad way to teach ethical theory is to present a complete ethical theory—normative ethics plus the preconditions of such (e.g., freedom) and other questions that arise about normative ethics (e.g, meaning)—offer the standard criticisms of that view, and then merely do the same thing for several other ethical theories. Students will come to believe moral philosophers were incompetents, or madmen, who wrote ethical theory. No view will be thought correct, for the teacher's criticisms will seem devastating and final. This problem is compounded by the portrayal by science teachers of the history of science as a march from ignorance to enlightenment. Philosophy and theology generally, and ethics more dramatically, then seem to students to be a march in circles.

At least two things can prevent this picture from capturing the minds of students: we can give them a better view of the history of science, and we can give them a better view of the history of ethical theory. The latter is made easier because most of the ethical theories we present are those which have stood the test of time. When this is pointed out, and some of the agreed-upon bad theories all are presented, some headway is made. For example, almost all philosophers and theologians are agreed that the Ten Commandments, *by themselves,* are not a complete and adequate normative ethical theory. Simple subjectivism, "An action is right when I believe it is right," is almost universally rejected. Bald evolutionism, "An action is right when it promotes the survival of higher organisms," has few supporters. Most of the "pop" theories are rejected by ethical theorists, and with good reason. We advise teachers to examine some of these theories, especially at the beginning of a course. This reassures students that their time will not be wasted, but that they will instead examine the theories that have fared best in the marketplace of ideas.

It is likely that every normative ethical theory chosen, no matter how bad it may be, will have had its defenders. This is a difference between science as an institution and philosophy and theology, the latter group usually being more tolerant toward those whose views are thought to be mistaken. It is a difference of degree, though, for there are many disagreements among scientists that continue. We thus arrive at the second strategy to offset the picture of science as a march to the truth in contrast to the muddling along of others. The history of science does not reveal such a march, and contemporary science reveals at least as much disagreement as normative ethics.[19] One favorite controversy concerns the Cartesians vs. the Newtonians on the question of action at a distance. Can one body influence another without an intervening medium? The Cartesians accused the Newtonians of postulating a mysterious force—gravity. Students usually turn out to be Cartesians on this point, and if you give them a choice, without identifying the good guys and the bad guys, most will side with the view that was eventually rejected. Each teacher will, naturally, choose his or her own favorite in the history of science. In addition, it is helpful to have one or two contemporary disagreements or puzzles in one's repertoire.

C. Tricksters

One problem faced by philosophers and theologians is that students often come to think of them as tricksters and, perhaps sophists, believing that teachers can make any view appear either bad or good because they are trained to do so. Students may conclude that their own view, which has just been shown to be inconsistent or to have seventeen, separate, fatal criticisms, is nevertheless correct. This attitude results, in part, from the mistaken view that pluralism requires an acceptance of all views as equally justified or correct. It also results, in part, from the metaethical view that ethics (and, perhaps, all philosophy) is "soft," just a subjective matter of selecting one view over another. Finally, students perceive, quite correctly, that training in the tasks of marshalling evidence and the evaluation of views makes the teacher a very difficult opponent to defeat.

Perhaps the primary way to overcome this problem is to avoid giving the impression that the teacher is an opponent. This goal, which is very difficult because of the inevitable disagreements that arise in the teaching of ethics, is well worth achieving. It can be done by failing to take any stand, but then students think that the teacher is wishy-washy or that all views are equally correct. A teacher can take a stand, but then claim that everyone has an equal right to his or her own opinion. This, however, simply confuses the distinction between pluralism and relativism. One way to convince students that the teacher is not an opponent is to indicate that we are considering theories and not people; we are engaged together in the enterprise of seeking a correct theory, or at least seeking the methods (reasoning, arguments, theory comparison) that will enable each of us to seek out the correct or best theory.

To help overcome the students' sense of being tricked, the teacher can present a problem or an issue concerning which the teacher does not have a solution. The teacher can present the issue, along with the proposed solutions or theories, and then try to show why each is unsatisfactory. This does not commit one to the view that there is no solution, indeed, one can always express confidence that a solution will be reached. It does give the students a sense, though, that the teacher is not omniscient.

D. Physical Factors

Another set of factors that determine how an ethics course will be taught is the size of the class, the class standing of students, prerequisites, and other ethics courses available. In large universities, ethics classes may have 250 or more students in a single class, while at smaller or more prosperous schools the same class may have but ten. In a class of 250 it will be much more difficult to make use of give-and-take discussion than in a class of ten, though it can be done. One can be informal about assignments, allow them to be changed significantly as interests develop in a small class, but that is very difficult in a large class. Cheating problems are more serious in large classes than in small, and class morale is often a serious problem in large classes.

E. Realities of Teaching Ethics

Why are some ethics courses so large? Departments need the enrollments to maintain budgets and staff. To teach the course that enrolls five, many departments find they must offer another that enrolls 250. Also, once a base rate is established, departments must continue to enroll at least that number of students or risk a cut in budget on the grounds of falling enrollment. Deans find this stance difficult to resist because they are constantly under pressure to cut costs.

If an ethics course is one in a sequence, or the base course for other ethics courses, this will influence what is taught. Most institutions have a course that introduces students to the main types of normative ethical theory. Students will learn what a normative ethical theory is, how to apply it, and how to evaluate it critically. In a terminal ethics course the survey of theories tends to be broader. If students are likely to take an advanced ethics course in which metaethical concerns are covered, that reduces coverage of those topics in the base course. If applied ethics courses are offered, this reduces the need for a range of applications to show how the theories work.

If there are no graduate courses in ethics at an institution, and a teacher has an interest in research in that field, it may lead to the introduction of some fairly esoteric topics in the undergraduate classroom. For example, a teacher might talk about Rawls's notion of the original position in a sophisticated way, follow it up with a comparison between it and ideal observer theories, and end with a positive view concerning principles of justice. There is nothing wrong with this as long as it does not replace the rest of the normative ethics that would have been taught in the course. Teaching is neither a one-way dishing-out of information to students, nor just an opportunity for a teacher to pursue his or her own research. Ideally it is a process of learning from which both teacher and student benefit. The teacher, in this role, is the leader or guide, much as Socrates thought of himself as a midwife for the ideas of his students. The service personnel model for faculty, which is frequently commended, works against this fruitful student-faculty interaction.

F. Academic Freedom and Unpopular Views

Two different academic freedom cases can arise in connection with the teaching of ethics. One occurs when a teacher holds a view that seems to preclude pluralism and engages in indoctrination to inculcate that view. The second can arise when someone is hired to teach at a school, usually a religious institution, which officially endorses a specific ethical theory.

Suppose, as one occasionally hears, a Marxist is teaching an ethics course to undergraduates. Suppose also that the teacher pushes this view, demeans all other views, doesn't allow other views to be given a fair hearing, and uses sophistic techniques to silence critics in the classroom. This person, we would argue, is not a competent teacher, not because of the Marxist view, but because of failure to meet the goals of teaching ethics. A charge of incompetence must be supported by evidence that concerns the teaching, not the view that is held by the instructor. Everyone who teaches ethics thinks that some normative ethical theory or other is better than the others, and he or she should be able to explain the supporting reasons whether the theory be utilitarian, Marxist, egoistic, or amoral.

The much more difficult case involves the institution with an official or even semiofficial point of view. On the one hand, it seems clear that once such an institution has hired a qualified individual to teach ethics, a person who did not hide his or her actual views in order to get the job, then academic freedom legitimately prevents the institution from dictating which view will come out "best" in the ethics class. On the other hand, if an institution explicitly decides to hire a person of a particular ethical persuasion (e.g., Marxist, Thomist, libertarian, or utilitarian), is such dictation morally or legally permissible? If the individual were to change beliefs and adjust the ethics course accordingly, does the institution then have grounds to fire that person without violating academic freedom?

G. Student Capacities

The widely discussed decline of students' abilities to read and write makes the assignment of reading materials in ethics courses difficult. Most teachers of a first course in ethics want students to read at least some original material in the history of ethics. As mentioned earlier, though philosophers think John Stuart Mill wrote very clear prose, students find Mill difficult and find other great moral philosophers even more so. This has led to a proliferation of less difficult works, many illustrated with cartoons, letters to the editor, and easy-to-read dramatic fiction.[20]

A related problem is the age of most undergraduates in ethics courses, usually between eighteen and twenty-one. Aristotle suggests that the study of ethics should not begin until after age thirty, for people do not have sufficient maturity and experience. Young students are frequently unsympathetic to those who act out of fear, from the employee who agrees to cover up illegal activities to the person who betrays comrades to save his or her own life. They also tend to believe that they, as individuals, are not susceptible to moral corruption and temptation. This is a difficult issue to address in class, but almost all who teach undergraduate ethics attempt to make students sensitive to additional issues, beyond their present experience.

H. Amoralism and Skepticism

Teachers of undergraduate ethics courses often notice very early that a significant portion of the class does not recognize that it makes moral judgments, acts on the basis of ethical evaluations, or is enmeshed in a moral environment. Sometimes students think that the claim "I (or anyone) believe that an action is right" has the same meaning as the claim that "An action is right." (While this equation can be used to express the sophisticated metaethical view of the noncognitivist, students usually do not use it that way.) Sometimes they suppose that there is no evidence available for moral claims, and that the only way to defeat moral skepticism is to equate the acceptance of a moral belief with its acceptability. Other students, seeing that the two are not generally the same, and thinking there is no way to show that one moral opinion is better than another, embrace amoralism; the view that nothing is right or wrong. Perhaps the most important way to overcome this problem is to discuss the actual moral problems that arise in the classroom. Another strategy is to set forth a number of normative ethical theories and show how their acceptability is dependent upon the critical apparatus that the students are acquiring.

Students will frequently say, "I don't use moral terms such as 'right' and 'wrong.' I like some things and don't like others, but there is no such thing as morality." This is, in part, a verbal matter, though again there may be a serious underlying philosophical issue. Students who say such things will also claim that we should or should not have restrictive laws concerning abortion, gun control, and drugs. When asked why, they do not respond with preferences, but instead give reasons. These reasons are just those that we all give to defend our moral views. In addition, it almost always turns out that the students hold some normative ethical theory and are actually using it in the presentation of the reasons. Unfortunately, students often make use of two or more incompatible theories at the same time. One of the tasks of teaching ethics is to show that the views are incompatible and why that is not something to be accepted lightly.

I. Pluralism and Relativism

We pride ourselves on having a pluralistic society in which many different cultural subgroups flourish. The mix of elements from different cultures helps to make our society interesting and gives it a vital mix of different ideas, cuisines, religions, music, literature, and dance. We tend to think that tolerance and appreciation of different cultures is the appropriate attitude and to condemn the view that one of the subcultures is inferior to another. The old melting pot idea was that each subculture would be swallowed up into a blend that would become American culture. The new "ethnic" idea seems to be that distinctness of cultural groups is a good thing to preserve, though those who wish to give up some aspect should be free to do so. We may indeed be evolving a common culture that contains elements from the various subcultures, but many of the subcultures have and should— so this view goes—remain distinct.

A problem in teaching ethics arises because of an ambiguous view of ethics and pluralism. Is a person's moral view (normative ethics) part of the subculture or is it something else? To focus the problem more clearly, consider the following two statements:

1. All moral claims are equally correct.

2. All (seriously held) moral claims have an equal right to be heard.

If, in the first statement, we substitute "subculture" for "moral claim" and "good" for "correct," then we have the claim of cultural pluralism. In fact, considered this way, there is no difference between (1) and (2) because (2) becomes the view that every subculture has an equal right to be maintained by its members. When we consider morality, though, the situation seems to be quite different. If the Male Chauvinist Society (a fictional group—so far) claims that women are and ought to be the servants of men, we feel free to reject this view as being *incorrect,* though most of us would support the right of this view to be *heard.* Slaveholders believed that keeping slaves was morally permissible. We are generally agreed that they were mistaken, even though it was no doubt true that within the subculture of the slaveholders it was thought to be morally permissible.

Philosophers give many explanations of the difference between (1) and (2), as do social scientists, theologians, politicians, and others. Some maintain that (1) is true; this is one version of ethical relativism, a view held by a small number of philosophers and theologians. Many students confuse cultural pluralism with ethical relativism. As a result, teachers of undergraduate ethics must attend to the distinction and convince students that it is neither un-American, antidemocratic nor antipluralistic to suggest that not all moral views are equally correct. Most teachers of ethics also emphasize that views have an equal right to be heard, that every student with a seriously held view has a right to have that view aired and examined.

We would extend the right to be heard to views of subcultures in our society, but insist that not every view is correct. For example, if many students and parents in a school system believe that specific creation and not evolution is the explanation of life in its present form, then that view should be covered in a biology course. At the same time, the biology teacher has a professional obligation to evaluate the competing theories presented. Every biological view that is important to the community has a right to be heard, but not all are equally correct. Professions other than philosophy and theology will have to learn to resist public pressures to label a view correct that in their own professional judgment is not correct.

J. Bad Courses and Enrollment

Gresham's Law in economics has it that bad money drives out good. Economists no doubt disagree about this, but the dispute in universities concerning good and bad courses is at least as hot and heavy. In most universities funds are distributed to colleges and departments, at least to some degree, on the basis of enrollment. Since most humanities departments have experienced enrollment declines, the money received by such units has been decreasing. In an attempt to bolster enrollments and thus to save jobs, various "glamour" courses have been offered. This has occurred in such departments as English, history, philosophy, languages, and religious studies. The grade requirements for these courses, according to some, have gone down; less work is required and what is done is graded in light of a lower standard. The resulting combination of grade inflation and quality deflation has made some humanities areas and ethics courses the object of scorn by people in other areas of the university. It is our impression this trend has, on the whole, been reversed. Administrators especially must be aware of this problem and the all-too-human tendency to try to protect jobs and "territory." To help prevent bad courses from driving out good, we must reward those who teach good courses, we must protect those areas whose good courses do not pay for themselves by enrollments, and perhaps we might think about restoring more required courses.

K. Problems and Techniques Concerning Disagreement

One problem in teaching ethics arises because of the importance of individual judgments and theories. Because the views are important ones, it is difficult for students to separate the critical analysis of a view from a critical attitude toward its holder. For example, one has to make clear that a criticism of egoism as an ethical theory is not a criticism of the person holding that theory. Those trained critically to evaluate a theory sometimes forget that others find it difficult to see that a person can be intelligent, discerning, and a good person even though his or her ethical theory is flawed. A helpful technique for overcoming this problem is to suggest a community discussion of a theory, e.g., egoism. Everyone is invited to defend the theory from the criticisms (or try to find them). By making it clear that those who offer defenses are not committed to the view, but are instead giving it a run for its money, we lift a burden from everyone. Of course one should not forbid people from identifying themselves as defenders of a view, for students should be encouraged to stand up for what they think is correct. But one also wants them to consider the main theories before they lock themselves into one position. By emphasizing the advantage of a tentative commitment to an ethical theory, one allows students to pursue the theory where it leads, but makes it easier to abandon views that are not defensible. This approach is helped by the tendency of students to be swayed by each theory they study. A prior warning of this tendency along with the recognition of it as a natural and common phenomenon, leads students to become more relaxed and intellectually flexible.

A closely related problem arises from stands on particular moral issues. For example, some students will think that women have an unqualified moral right to an abortion in the first trimester. Others will think that abortion on demand in the first trimester is not morally permissible, even though some abortions, e.g., when the life of the mother is endangered, may be morally permitted and justified. These disputes are valuable because they make for lively discussions, show the relevance of the various normative ethical theories, and show students that they have a stake in moral issues. However, if the discussion leads to a polarization, hardens attitudes, and gives the impression that moral disputes are not resolvable by rational means, then, in our view, such disputes would have an overall negative impact on the course. So, the question is, how do we get out the valuable aspects of discussion of controversial issues and at the same time prevent the bad aspects? Needless to say there are a variety of different approaches, some of which we approve of and others of which we do not.

One method used with success is to apply various normative theories, e.g., utilitarianism and egoism, and show how the application of each of those would change the context of the discussion. This tends to make the discussion more rational, though students are sometimes confused by how the same theory, say utilitarianism, can be used to support both sides of a moral issue. Another method is for the teacher to provide leadership for tolerance of other views, part of what we call pluralism. The danger here is that while we want to tolerate disagreement and even encourage it as indicated above, we do not want to give the impression that both parties to the dispute are correct. They may both be mistaken about the issue, but it cannot be that both are correct. (It should be kept in mind that there are certain metaethical theories that hold either that there is no such thing as a correct moral judgment, or that all moral judgments sincerely held are equally correct. It is here assumed that those theories are not correct.) It is tempting for an ethics teacher simply to elicit the opposing views and leave students with the impression that nothing more can be done.

One technique used at Ohio State for this problem with apparent success is called *moral negotiation*. The specific moral issue is first carefully described, as was done above, by saying that we are concerned with abortion on demand in the first trimester. The aim is to make the issue specific and determinate enough to allow a fruitful disagreement. When discussing abortion, for example, almost everyone in the class would agree there are circumstances in which abortion is not morally justified (e.g., in the ninth month in order to injure the father) and other circumstances in which it is morally justified (e.g., the mother's life is endangered and the fetus is known to have a serious genetic disorder such as Down's Syndrome). What we have to do is find the description of the situation that reflects the disagreement rather than hides it, and clarifies it rather than obscures it. It happens not infrequently that simply getting clear on the moral issue resolves it, an occurrence that demonstrates the importance of clarity. This, too, is an important lesson, for the teacher of ethics frequently spends a great deal of time attempting to make clearer, claims and theories that students sometimes think are clear already, or that everyone "really" understands without need for clarification.

After the clarification of the problem, the next step is to ask persons on both sides of the question to present the reasons for each opposing side. No one is asked to take a stand on the moral issue at that time, only to present his or her reasons or those he or she has heard other persons present for the two sides. Those who are undecided can enter into this as easily as those who are firmly convinced they have the correct view. The reasons are all listed in the form of two conditional statements, statements of an if-then form. Two typical conditional statements might be as follows:

1. If abortion on demand in the first trimester
   a. tends to reduce respect for human life, and
   b. makes more likely killing of human beings in social contexts, and
   c. consists of killing a being with full human rights (either because of a religious position or a view of when rights begin),

   then

   d. abortion on demand in the first trimester is not morally justified.

2. If abortion on demand in the first trimester
   a'. does not significantly reduce respect for human life, and,
   b'. on the whole prevents harm to pregnant women who have the abortion (mostly psychological or social), and
   c'. does not consist in killing a being with full human rights (this is usually held on the grounds that rights are acquired gradually, and that although a first trimester fetus may have some rights they are slight at that time),

   then
   d'. abortion on demand in the first trimester is morally justified.

In a typical discussion there would be many more items included, as one may imagine, and a good deal of discussion about what some items mean. Some of the items are themselves moral items, e.g., the rights claims, and these have to be specially noted. Since most students will have taken part in discussions concerning abortion it will be assumed that there is no problem in understanding that this is a selection of reasons given.

At this point, having presented the reasons that persons on both sides give, we are working cooperatively. Each side is invited to provide reasons given to support the abortion on demand claim, and also to give reasons to support the denial of that claim. The enterprise is a cooperative one even though individuals disagree on which of the moral judgments—the statements that follow the "then" in the if-then statement—is correct. Once the statements are constructed, the question is asked if everyone agrees with *both* of the if-then statements. Usually, at this point, some will say that they do disagree. Most of these students, though, will base their disagreement on the fact that they disagree with one or more of the statements in the antecedents of the if-then statements, the statements that are labeled (a), (b), (c). However, it is relatively easy to point out that we frequently think that some if-then statements are acceptable whose antecedents we believe to be false. Again, we may think both the antecedents and the consequent (the statement that follows "then") are false and yet the entire statement is true. For example, we might think that "If Kennedy does not run, then Carter will get the nomination," is true, even though we think that Kennedy will run and that Carter will not get the nomination. More fancifully, we think it is true that "If Kennedy becomes king then democracy will disappear from the United States" even though we don't think that Kennedy will become king. It is *on the assumption that* or *conditionally that* we can and do agree with both conditional statements.

As a result of the conditional agreement the atmosphere of the disagreement changes. Both sides now realize that the other side has grounds for its views. They both realize that the heart of the disagreement concerns the items in the antecedent. The conditional agreement establishes for each side the moral credentials of the other—each can see the opponent as morally sensitive, people they would agree with but for the disagreement concerning the antecedent. Most of the items in the antecedent are, at least in a broad sense, factual matters, so the sense of being equally "good" morally is given an added boost. By using this method, hostility is reduced and the discussion comes to focus on the factual disagreements that tend to underlie moral disagreement.

There are many other things one can do with this method, as has been described elsewhere.[21] Enough has been said here, though, to give an idea of how the method can be used. It is a simple method, though it may sound complex when described; people who try it report they have no difficulty in adapting it to their own style of teaching.

L. Resource Material

Reading material can be divided into three kinds, original sources, anthologies, and texts.[22] Original materials are the works of the recognized great thinkers in ethics. Almost always a teacher will use more than one of these works: frequently three or more will be used to show a range of different views. Here is a selection of such authors and the typical works used:

Plato, *Republic, Protagoras, Phaedo, Gorgias, Apology, Crito.*
Aristotle, *Nicomachean Ethics, Politics*
Lucretius (as a representative epicurean), *On the Nature of Things*
Marcus Aurelius (as a representative stoic), *The Meditations*
Augustine, *Confessions, The City of God, Enchiridian, On Freedom of the Will.* (Selections from these works are chosen.)
Aquinas, *Summa Theologica, Summa Contra Gentile.* (Appropriate selections are taken from these works.)
Hobbes, Thomas, *Leviathan.*
Cudworth, Ralph, *Eternal and Immutable Morality.*
Spinoza, Benedict, *Ethics.*
Hutcheson, Francis, *System of Moral Philosophy.*
Butler, Bishop Joseph, *Five Sermons,* "A Dissertation Upon the Nature of Virtue."
Hume, David, *An Enquiry Concerning the Principles of Morals; A Treatise of Human Nature.* (Appropriate selections are taken from these works, especially the *Treatise.*)
Voltaire, *Candide, Zadig, Philosophical Dictionary.*
Rousseau, Jean-Jacques, *The Social Contract, Emile.*
Kant, Immanuel, *Foundations of the Metaphysics of Morals, Critique of Practical Reason.*
Bentham, Jeremy, *Principles of Morals and Legislation.*
Mill, John Stuart, *Utilitarianism, On Liberty.*
Hegel, G. W. F., *Philosophy of Right.*

After Hegel we reach the twentieth-century period, where disagreement about who is important is stronger. A variety of works from various perspectives, Marxist, existentialist, Christian, pragmatic, and analytic are available. In addition to the use of works listed as separate volumes, many of these same works or parts thereof have been anthologized. Let us turn our attention first to anthologies. There are at least three different kinds of anthologies available for the undergraduate market: relevant topics, long selections, and short philosophical selections. The "relevance" anthologies, of which there are a large number, contain selections that provide arguments or positions for or against the pressing moral issues of the day. Obvious examples of this sort are John Ladd's *Ethical Issues Relating to Life and Death* and Richard Wasserstrom's *Today's Moral Problems* (2nd ed.). In the latter, the section titles are "Privacy," "Abortion," "Racism and Sexism," "Sexual Morality," "Punishment," "The Obligation to Obey the Law," and "Violence, Nonviolence, and War." Almost all the articles in this anthology were written within the last ten years.

The long anthology is represented by Andrew Oldenquist's *Readings in Moral Philosophy.* There are sizable or complete selections from Plato, *The Republic;* Aristotle, *Nicomachean Ethics;* Joseph Butler, *Fifteen Sermons;* David Hume, *A Treatise of Human Nature;* Immanuel Kant, *Fundamental Principles of the Metaphysics of Morals;* J. S. Mill, *Utilitarianism;* G. E. Moore, *Ethics;* A. J. Ayer, *Language, Truth and Logic;* and S. E. Toulmin, *An Examination of the Place of Reason in Ethics.* Another anthology of this kind is *Readings in Ethics,* edited by Gordon H. Clark and T. V. Smith.

The third kind of anthology is represented by Marcus G. Singer, *Morals and Values,* as well as W. K. Frankena and John T. Granrose, *Introductory Readings in Ethics,* and Richard Brandt's *Value and Obligation.* The attempt here is to provide examples of philosophical reasoning, usually not directly on particular topics such as abortion, but on theories as to how this reasoning properly occurs. The selections are not only on the nature of a correct or justified judgment, but also contain philosophical advice on how to arrive at such judgment.

Which of these three kinds of anthology is most useful depends, of course, on what the teacher wants to do. Our own view is that the "relevance" anthologies contain less interesting philosophical material than the other two sorts, for the selections are usually too directly tied to the problem at hand so that no general philosophical lessons or skills are imparted. The longer anthologies contain selections difficult for students to understand because of the subtle way thinkers such as Kant and Aristotle weave together many topics. These can be used, but again the general philosophical lessons are more difficult to impart.

One problem about general lessons to be learned and skills to be imparted is that either the author or the teacher has to provide the connections between selections, make the categories in the parts clear, and show how the various authors are all involved in the same dialectical process. Many who prefer to use texts rather than anthologies give as a reason that students do not have this problem of making connections since, in the better texts, the connections are made by the same author who is discussing the issues. Ethics is a theoretical discipline concerned, in part, with moral problems. The concern has to be understood via the ethical questions that are asked, and moral problems have to be understood primarily through examples. The latter technique is acceptable, though the teacher will have to supplement the examples, for students are often unclear about what a moral problem is.

Most texts and anthologies are designed for introductory to middle level courses. The difference between teaching an introductory course and a middle level course does not have to be reflected in the material, but does have to be reflected in what the teacher takes for granted and what the teacher has to supply in each instance. In an elementary course the teacher has to supply the basic framework for doing any philosophy of ethics at all, for students have many misconceptions and usually have no good idea of what a philosopher or a theologian does. At the middle level one can assume the students are more knowledgeable, both with respect to philosophy and with respect to related material. They will have read more about history and will have had more experiences of their own from which they can draw to apply to the views under consideration.

A major reason for using texts, some with selections of readings and some not, is the common framework that is provided. Students have difficulty moving from the language of one author to that of another, so the problem can be solved by providing a single language. Some of the texts attempt to describe the major normative ethical theories in their own terms or with short quotes, and some include fairly lengthy selections.

Five representative textbooks that take different approaches are John Hospers, *Human Conduct;* Bernard Gert, *The Moral Rules;* Paul Taylor, *Principles of Ethics;* William Frankena, *Ethics,* and Bernard Rosen, *Strategies of Ethics.* Each of the authors covers the main normative ethical theories, provides criticisms, and takes a stand. The stand usually consists of the defense of one of the main normative theories or some variations of it, though the primary purpose of the text is in no case the defense of the view chosen. Depending on the class and how much time one has, an anthology or some selection of works of important authors can be used along with such texts.

This brief section on what is used in teaching concludes with a description of two different ethics courses taught by Bernard Rosen at two different institutions. First, an honors course in ethics, which was taught at the University of Western Ontario, consisted of fifteen students, not all of whom were majors. The course lasted the entire year, and met three times a week for a total of about twenty-three weeks. Readings consisted of Rosen's *Strategies of Ethics,* an anthology, and Brandt's *Value and Obligation,* and each student had to choose a major work by a major author from a list very much like the one presented in the first part of this section. The course covered the principal views via the "single voice" of the text, compared the presentation with the author's own way of stating the view in the anthology, and then the students wrote a lengthy paper in which they pointed out the shortcomings or additional points about their chosen author. There were quizzes and such during the year, but the main method of testing was by means of first a short and then a long paper.

This course was the most satisfying undergraduate ethics course taught by Rosen in a regular university setting. The students learned a great deal, the teacher got to know them all well, they felt free to discuss issues in class, and everyone felt good about the course.

In sharp contrast is the second kind of course, the typical lecture ethics course Rosen teaches at Ohio State. Some of the ethics courses are taught in smaller (up to 40) classes, but the lecture typically enrolls around 250. The quarter is ten weeks long, and the students attend lectures three times a week and a recitation section (with graduate teaching associates) twice a week. In such a course a text is typically assigned, usually Rosen, and about two thirds of it is covered. Students write short papers, take quizzes, and write a final paper. The short papers have to be carefully designed so as to make it possible both for the students to have a valuable learning experience and for the teaching assistants to grade them. The quizzes are all multiple choice and usually constructed by the instructor. The final paper allows the students to begin a defense of the normative ethical theory he or she is inclined to hold. The course has to be carefully planned before the quarter begins; a calendar detailing assignments and due dates is passed out the first day of class and is followed closely unless some emergency occurs.

This course is challenging to teach, and it is satisfying to discover how much can be learned by students in such a course. From the perspective of the teacher, large lecture courses are needed to fill a commitment to provide an education for all those who are able and desire it. Most of those instructors who teach the lecture ethics course work very hard to make it valuable for the students. On the whole, it would seem that they succeed, though the effort needed to work with 250 students in ten weeks is enormously greater than that needed to succeed with a smaller number of students over a longer period of time.

Notes

1. Douglas Sloan, "History of the Teaching of Ethics in American Higher Education," Daniel Callahan and Sissela Bok, eds., in *Ethics Teaching in Higher Education* (New York: Plenum Press, 1980).

2. Ibid.

3. See, for example, A. J. Ayer, "Critique of Ethics and Theology," chap. 6, *Language, Truth and Logic,* 2nd ed. (New York: Dover Publications, 1946).

4. See, for example, W. D. Hudson, *Modern Moral Philosophy* (New York: Anchor Books, 1970). This book surveys moral philosophy through the 1960s and finds almost nothing but metaethics.

5. For a good overview of the development and decline of logical positivism, see John Passmore, chap. 16, "Logical Positivism," *A Hundred Years of Philosophy,* 2nd ed. (Middlesex, England: Penguin Books Ltd., 1968).

6. Institute on Human Values in Medicine, *Human Values Teaching Programs for Health Professionals: Self-Descriptive Reports From Twenty-Nine Schools,* 3rd ed. (Philadelphia: Society for Health and Human Values, 1976).

7. American Association for the Advancement of Science, *EVIST Resource Directory* (Washington: Office of Science Education, 1978); and Ezra D. Heitowit, Janet Epstein, and Gerald Steinberg, *Science, Technology, and Society: A Guide to the Field* (Ithaca: Cornell University Press, 1976).

8. These views range from those who think a complete course in ethical theory should be a prerequisite for any applied ethics course to those who think at least a few weeks of each applied ethics course should concern ethical theory.

9. See, for example, James Rachels, ed., *Moral Problems: A Collection of Philosophical Essays* (New York: Harper & Row, 1971).

10. See, for example, Tom Beauchamp and Leroy Walters, eds., *Contemporary Issues in Bioethics* (Belmont, Calif.: Dickenson Publishing Co., 1978); and Robert Hunt and John Arras, eds., *Ethical Issues in Modern Medicine* (Palo Alto: Mayfield Publishing Co., 1977).

11. See, for example, Gilbert Harmon, *The Nature of Morality* (New York: Oxford University Press, 1977).

12. See Daniel Callahan, "Goals in the Teaching of Ethics," in Callahan and Bok, eds., *Ethics Teaching*. . . . (New York: Plenum Press, 1980).

13. See, for example, Howard Kirschenbaum, Sidney Simon, and Leland Howe, *Values Clarification* (New York: Hart Publishing Co., 1972).

14. See Daniel Callahan, "Qualifications for the Teaching of Ethics," in Callahan and Bok, eds., *Ethics Teaching*. . . (New York: Plenum Press, 1980).

15. Ibid.

16. See J. R. Rest, "Recent Research on an Objective Test of Moral Judgment: How the Important Issues of a Moral Dilemma are Defined," in D. J. DePalma and J. M. Foley, eds., *Moral Development: Current Theory and Research* (Hillsdale, Calif.: Erlbaum, 1975).

17. John Dewey, "Moral Principles in Education," in *John Dewey: The Middle Works,* vol. 4, 1907–1909 (Carbondale and Edwardsville, Ill.: Southern Illinois University Press, 1977), p. 274.

18. See, for example, Bernard Rosen, *Strategies of Ethics* (Boston: Houghton Mifflin, 1978), chap. 3.

19. See, for example, John Theodore Merz, *A History of European Scientific Thought in the Nineteenth Century* (New York: Dover Publications, Inc., 1965).

20. The best of such works, and one that contains many useful pieces, is Robert Baum, ed., *Ethical Arguments for Analysis,* 2nd ed. (New York: Holt, Rinehart and Winston, New York, 1976).

21. See Rosen, *Strategies of Ethics,* pp. 148–61.

22. Parts of this section are from a review that appeared in *Teaching Philosophy* 2, nos. 3, 4 (September, 1978). Our thanks to *Teaching Philosophy* for permission to use those parts.

Bibliography

I. General Books and Articles on the Teaching of Ethics

Archambault, Reginald D. "Criteria for Success in Moral Instruction." *Harvard Educational Review* 33 (Fall 1963): 472–83.

Bennett, William J. and Delattre, Edwin. "Moral Education in the Schools." *The Public Interest,* no. 50 (Winter 1978): 81–98.

Bereiter, Carl. "The Morality of Moral Education." *Hastings Center Report* 8:2 (April, 1978): 20–25.

Bok, Derek. "Can Ethics Be Taught?" *Change* 8 (October 1976): 26–30.

Bok, Sissela and Callahan, Daniel. "Teaching Applied Ethics." *Radcliffe Quarterly* 69:2 (June, 1979): 30–33.

Callahan, Daniel and Bok, Sissela, eds. *Ethics Teaching in Higher Education.* New York, Plenum Press, 1980.

Frankena, William. "Towards a Philosophy of Moral Education." *Harvard Educational Review* 28 (Fall 1958): 300–13.

Montefiore, Alan. "Moral Philosophy and the Teaching of Morality." *Harvard Educational Review* 35 (1965): pp. 435–49.

Ozar, David. "Teaching Philosophy and Teaching Values." *Teaching Philosophy* 2, no. 3 (1979): 1–10.

Peters, R. S. "Moral Development and Moral Learning." *Monist* 58 (1974): 541–68.

Ryle, Gilbert. "Can Virtue Be Taught?" in R. F. Dearden, P. H. Hirst, and R. S. Peters. *Education and the Development of Reason.* London: Routledge and Kegan Paul, 1972.

The Teaching of Ethics in Higher Education: A Report by The Hastings Center. Hastings-on-Hudson, N.Y.: The Hastings Center, 1980.

Trow, Martin. "Higher Education and Moral Development." *American Association of University Professors. Bulletin* (Spring 1976), pp. 20–27.

Walzer, Michael. "Teaching Morality." *The New Republic,* June 10, 1978, pp. 12–14.

II. Moral Philosophy

Baier, Kurt. *The Moral Point of View: A Rational Basis of Ethics.* New York: Random House, 1968.

Berlin, Isaiah. *Four Essays on Liberty.* Oxford: Oxford University Press, 1969.

Bok, Sissela. *Lying: Moral Choice in Public and Private Life.* New York: Pantheon Books, 1978.

Brandt, Richard B. *Ethical Theory.* Englewood Cliffs, N.J.: Prentice-Hall, 1959.

———. *Value and Obligation.* New York: Harcourt Brace Jovanovich, 1961.

Cavell, Stanley. *The Claim of Reason.* New York: Oxford University Press, 1979.

Donagan, Alan. *The Theory of Morality.* Chicago: University of Chicago Press, 1977.

Feinberg, Joel, ed. *Moral Concepts.* New York: Oxford University Press, 1969.

Foot, Phillippa. *Virtues and Vices and Other Essays in Moral Philosophy.* Berkeley: University of California Press, 1979.

Frankena, William K. *Ethics.* 2nd ed. Englewood Cliffs, N.J.: Prentice-Hall, 1974.

——— and Granrose, John T. *Introductory Readings in Ethics.* Englewood Cliffs, N.J.: Prentice-Hall, 1974.

Fried, Charles. *Right and Wrong.* Cambridge, Mass.: Harvard University Press, 1978.

Gert, Bernard. *The Moral Rules.* New York: Harper & Row, 1970.

Gewirth, Alan. *Reason and Morality.* Chicago: University of Chicago Press, 1978.

Harmon, Gilbert. *The Nature of Morality.* New York: Oxford University Press, 1977.

Hospers, John. *Human Conduct: Problems of Ethics.* New York: Harcourt Brace Jovanovich, 1972.

MacIntyre, Alasdair. *A Short History of Ethics.* New York: Macmillan, 1966.

Mackie, J. L. *Ethics: Inventing Right and Wrong.* New York: Penguin, 1977.

Nozick, Robert. *Anarchy, State, and Utopia.* New York: Basic Books, 1974.

Oldenquist, Andrew. *Readings in Moral Philosophy.* Boston: Houghton Mifflin, 1961.

Rachels, James, ed. *Moral Problems: A Collection of Philosophical Essays.* New York: Harper & Row, 1971.

Rawls, John. *A Theory of Justice.* Cambridge, Mass.: Harvard University Press, 1971.

Rosen, Bernard. *Strategies of Ethics.* Boston: Houghton Mifflin, 1978.

Sellars, W. S. and Hospers, John, eds. *Readings in Ethical Theory.* 2nd edition. New York: Appleton-Century-Crofts, 1970.

Singer, Marcus G. *Morals and Values.* New York: Charles Scribner's Sons, 1977.

Smart, J. J. C. and Williams, Bernard. *Utilitarianism: For and Against.* New York: Cambridge University Press, 1973.

Taylor, Paul W. *Principles of Ethics: An Introduction.* Belmont, Calif.: Dickenson Publishing Co., 1971.

————, ed. *Problems in Moral Philosophy: An Introduction to Ethics.* 2nd edition. Belmont, California: Dickenson Publishing Co., 1971.

Toulmin, Stephen Edelston. *An Examination of the Place of Reason in Ethics.* New York: Cambridge University Press, 1950.

Wasserstrom, Richard. *Today's Moral Problems.* 2nd ed. New York: Macmillan, 1979.

Wellman, Carl. *Morals and Ethics.* Glenview, Ill.: Scott, Foresman & Co., 1975.

Williams, Bernard. *Morality: An Introduction to Ethics.* New York: Harper & Row, 1972.

III. Theological Ethics

Fox, Marvin, ed. *Modern Jewish Ethics: Theory and Practice.* Columbus, Ohio: Ohio State University Press, 1975.

Gustafson, James. *Protestant and Roman Catholic Ethics.* Chicago: University of Chicago Press, 1978.

————. *Can Ethics Be Christian?* Chicago: University of Chicago Press, 1975.

Gutierrez, Gustavo. *A Theology of Liberation.* Maryknoll, N.Y.: Orbis Books, 1973.

Häring, Bernard. *Toward a Christian Moral Theology.* Notre Dame, Ind.: University of Notre Dame Press, 1966.

Kellner, Menachem Marc, ed. *Contemporary Jewish Ethics*. New York: Sanhedrin Press, 1978.

Maguire, Daniel C. *The Moral Choice*. Garden City, N.Y.: Doubleday, 1978.

McCormick, Richard A. *Ambiguity in Moral Choice*. Milwaukee: Marquette University Press, 1973.

Niebuhr, H. Richard. *The Responsible Self*. New York: Harper & Row, 1978.

Niebuhr, Reinhold. *An Interpretation of Christian Ethics*. Cleveland: World Publishing Co., 1963 (1935).

O'Connell, Timothy E. *Principles for a Catholic Morality*. New York: Seabury Press, 1978.

Outka, Gene H. *Agape: An Ethical Analysis*. New Haven: Yale University Press, 1972.

Quinn, Philip L. *Divine Commands and Moral Requirements*. New York: Oxford University Press, 1978.

Ramsey, Paul. *Basic Christian Ethics*. Chicago: University of Chicago Press, 1950.

Tillich, Paul. *Morality and Beyond*. New York: Harper & Row, 1963.

IV. Education and Morality

Astin, Alexander. *Four Critical Years: Effects of College on Beliefs, Attitudes and Knowledge*. San Francisco: Jossey-Bass, 1977.

Beck, C. M., Crittenden, B. S., and Sullivan, E. V., eds. *Moral Education*. Toronto: University of Toronto Press, 1971.

Bruneau, William. "A Resource Bibliography for the History of Moral Education in Western Europe 1850–1939." *Moral Education Forum* 4:3 (Fall 1979): 8–15, 18–20.

Carter, Jack L. "The Anatomy of Controversy: Freedom and Responsibility for Teaching." *Bioscience* 29:8 (August, 1979): 481–84.

Delattre, Edwin J. and Bennett, William J. "Where the Values Movement Goes Wrong." *Change* 11:1 (February 1979): pp. 38–43.

Gordon, David. "Free-Will and the Undesirability of Moral Education." *Educational Theory* 25 (1975): pp. 407–16.

Grant, Gerald and Riesman, David. *The Perpetual Dream: Reform and Experiment in the American College*. Chicago: The University of Chicago Press, 1978.

Hall, Robert T. and Davis, John V. *Moral Education in Theory and Practice*. Buffalo, N.Y.: Prometheus Books, 1975.

Hamm, C. M. "The Content of Moral Education, or in Defense of the 'Bag of Virtues'." *School Review* 85 (1977): 218–28.

Hyman, H. H. and Wright, C. R. *Education's Lasting Influence on Values.* Chicago: University of Chicago Press, 1979.

Kirschenbaum, Howard, Simon, Sidney, and Howe, Leland. *Values Clarification.* New York: Hart Publishing Co., 1972.

Kohlberg, Lawrence. *Collected Papers on Moral Development and Moral Education.* Cambridge, Mass.: Center for Moral Education, Harvard University, 1973.

Langford, Glenn, ed. *New Essays in the Philosophy of Education.* London: Routledge and Kegan Paul, 1973.

Lickona, Thomas, ed. *Moral Development and Behavior.* New York: Holt, Rinehart, and Winston, 1976.

McGrath, Earl J. *Values, Liberal Education and National Destiny.* Indianapolis: Lilly Endowment, n.d.

Middleberg, M. I. "Moral Education and the Liberal Arts." *Educational Record* 57 (1976): 236–40.

Mischel, Theodore. *Cognitive Development and Epistemology.* New York: Academic Press, 1971.

Perry, William G. *Forms of Intellectual and Ethical Development in the College Years: A Scheme.* New York: Holt, Rinehart, and Winston, 1970.

Peters, R. S., ed. *The Philosophy of Education.* Oxford: Oxford University Press, 1971.

Rosen, B. "Moral Education and Moral Theory." *Teaching Philosophy* 1 (1976): 401–21.

Rudolph, Frederick. *Curriculum: A History of the American Undergraduate Course of Study Since 1636.* San Francisco: Jossey-Bass, 1972.

Schwarzlose, Richard A. "Socratic Method Adds Zest to Ethics, Law Classes." *Journalism Educator* 33:1 (April, 1978): 9–24.

Scriven, Michael. "Cognitive Moral Education." *Phi Delta Kappan* 56 (1975): 689–94.

V. Professional and Applied Ethics

Ackerman, Robert and Bauer, Raymond, eds. *Corporate Social Responsiveness: The Modern Dilemma.* Reston, Va.: Reston Publishing Company, Inc., 1976.

Barach, Jeffrey, ed. *The Individual, Business, and Society.* Englewood Cliffs, N.J.: Prentice-Hall, 1977.

Baum, Robert J. and Flores, Albert W., eds. *Ethical Problems in Engineering.* Troy, N.Y.: Rensselaer Polytechnic Institute, Human Dimensions Center, 1978.

Beauchamp, Tom L., ed. *Ethics and Public Policy.* N.J.: Prentice-Hall, 1975.

———— and Bowie, Norman, ed. *Ethical Theory and Business.* Englewood Cliffs, N.J.: Prentice-Hall, 1979.

———— and Childress, J. F. *Principles of Biomedical Ethics.* New York: Oxford University Press, 1979.

———— and Walters, LeRoy, ed. *Contemporary Issues in Bioethics.* Belmont, Calif.: Dickenson Publishing Co., 1978.

Bermant, Gordon, Kelman, Herbert, and Warwick, Donald, eds. *The Ethics of Social Intervention.* Washington, D.C.: Hemisphere Publishing Co., 1978.

Bledstein, Burton. *The Culture of Professionalism.* New York: W. W. Norton, 1976.

Boley, Bruno A. *Crossfire in Professional Education: Students, the Professions, and Society.* New York: Pergamon Press, 1977.

Bonnell, John A., ed. *A Guide for Developing Courses in Engineering.* NSPE Publication #2010, Washington, D.C.: National Society of Professional Engineers, 1976.

Bower, Robert T. and de Gasparis, Priscilla. *Ethics in Social Research: Protecting the Interests of Human Subjects.* New York: Praeger, 1978.

Calabresi, Guido and Bobbitt, Philip. *Tragic Choices.* New York: W. W. Norton, 1978.

Christians, Clifford G. "Fifty Years of Scholarship in Media Ethics." *Journal of Communication* 27 (Autumn, 1977): 19–29.

Cohen, Marshall et al., eds. *Equality and Preferential Treatment.* Princeton: Princeton University Press, 1976.

Davis, Ann and Aroskar, Mila. *Ethical Dilemmas and Nursing Practice.* New York: Appleton-Century-Crofts, 1978.

DeGeorge, Richard T. and Pichler, Joseph. *Ethics, Free Enterprise, and Public Policy: Original Essays on Moral Issues in Business.* Oxford: Oxford University Press, 1978.

Denzin, N. K. and Erikson, Kai. "On the Ethics of Disguised Observation." *Social Problems* 15 (1968): 502–6.

Diener, Edward and Crandall, Rick. *Ethics in Social and Behavioral Research.* Chicago: University of Chicago Press, 1978.

Donaldson, Thomas, and Werhane, Patricia, eds. *Ethical Issues in Business: A Philosophical Approach.* Englewood Cliffs, N.J.: Prentice-Hall, 1979.

Ethics, Professionalism & Maintaining Competence: Proceedings of a Conference held at the Ohio State University, March 10–11, 1977. New York: American Society of Civil Engineers, 1977.

Florman, Samuel. *The Existential Pleasures of Engineering.* New York: St. Martin's Press, 1976.

Freedman, Benjamin. "A Meta-Ethics for Professional Morality." *Ethics* 89, no. 1 (October, 1978): 1–19.

Freidson, Eliot. *Professional Dominance: The Social Structure of Medical Care.* New York: Atherton Press, 1970.

Fruchtbaum, Harold, ed. *The Social Responsibility of Engineers* (Annals of the New York Academy of Sciences: vol. 196, pt. 10). New York: Scholarly Reprints, 1973.

Glover, Jonathan. *Causing Deaths and Saving Lives.* New York: Penguin, 1971.

Gorovitz, Samuel et al., eds. *Moral Problems in Medicine.* Englewood Cliffs, N.J.: Prentice-Hall, 1976.

Hampshire, Stuart, ed. *Public and Private Morality.* Cambridge: Cambridge University Press, 1978.

Heitowit, Ezra D., Epstein, Janet, and Steinberg, Gerald. *Science, Technology, and Society: A Guide to the Field.* Ithaca, N.Y.: Cornell University Press, 1976.

Hendrix, Jon R. "A Survey of Bioethics Courses in U. S. Colleges and Universities." *American Biology Teacher* 39 (February, 1977): 85–92.

Humber, James M. and Almeder, Robert F., eds. *Biomedical Ethics and the Law.* New York: Plenum Press, 1976.

Hunt, Robert and Arras, John, eds. *Ethical Issues in Modern Medicine.* Palo Alto, Calif.: Mayfield Publishing Co., 1977.

Jonsen, Albert and Butler, L. H. "Public Ethics and Policymaking." *Hastings Center Report* 5:3 (August, 1975): 19–31.

Katz, Jay. *Experimentation with Human Beings: The Authority of the Investigator, Subject, Professions, and State in the Human Experimentation Process.* New York: Russell Sage Foundation, 1972.

Kelman, Herbert: *A Time to Speak: On Human Values and Social Research.* San Francisco: Jossey-Bass, 1968.

Ladd, John, ed. *Ethical Issues Relating to Life and Death.* New York: Oxford University Press, 1979.

Larson, Magali S. *The Rise of Professionalism.* Berkeley: University of California Press, 1977.

Layton, Edwin T., Jr. *Revolt of the Engineers: Social Responsibility and the American Engineering Profession.* Cleveland: Case Western Reserve Press, 1971.

Luthans, Fred and Hodgetts, Richard M., eds. *Social Issues in Business*. New York: Macmillan, 1976.

Merton, Robert K., ed. *Authority and the Individual*. New York: Arno Press, 1974.

Nicholson, Edward A., Litschert, Robert J., and Anthony, William P., eds. *Business Responsibility and Social Issues*. Columbus, Ohio: Charles E. Merrill Publishing Co., 1974.

Ramsey, Paul. *The Patient as Person*. New Haven: Yale University Press, 1970.

Reich, Warren T., editor-in-chief. *Encyclopedia of Bioethics*. New York: The Free Press, 1978.

Rivers, William L. and Schramm, Wilbur. *Responsibility in Mass Communication*. Revised Edition. New York: Harper & Row (1957), 1969.

Rivlin, Alice M. and Timpane, P. Michael, eds. *Ethical and Legal Issues of Social Experimentation*. Washington, D.C.: Brookings Institution, 1975.

Rubin, Bernard, ed. *Questioning Media Ethics*. New York: Praeger Special Studies, 1978.

Sethi, S. Prakash. *Up Against the Corporate Wall*. Englewood Cliffs, N.J.: Prentice-Hall, 1977.

Sjoberg, Gideon, ed. *Ethics, Politics, and Social Research*. San Francisco: Jossey-Bass, 1968.

Sollitto, Sharmon, Veatch, Robert, and Singer, Ira. *Bibliography of Society, Ethics, and the Life Sciences 1979–80*. Hastings-on-Hudson, N.Y.: The Hastings Center, 1979.

Steiner, George A. and Steiner, John F., eds. *Issues in Business and Society*. New York: Random House, 1972.

Swain, Bruce M. *Reporter's Ethics*. Ames, Iowa: Iowa State University Press, 1978.

Thayer, Lee, ed. *Communication: Ethical and Moral Issues*. New York: Gordon and Breach, 1973.

The Teaching of Bioethics: Report of the Commission on the Teaching of Bioethics. Hastings-on-Hudson, N.Y.: Institute of Society, Ethics and the Life Sciences, 1976.

Tribe, Laurence. *When Values Conflict: Essays on Environmental Analysis, Discourse and Decision*. Cambridge, Mass.: Ballinger, 1976.

Veatch, Robert. *Case Studies in Medical Ethics*. Cambridge, Mass.: Harvard University Press, 1977.

Walters, LeRoy, ed. *Bibliography of Bioethics*. Detroit: Gale Research Co., 1973.

Walzer, Michael. *Just and Unjust Wars.* New York: Basic Books, 1977.

Weil, Vivian M. "Moral Issues in Engineering: An Engineering School Instructional Approach." *Professional Engineer.* October, 1977, pp. 45–47.

Wolin, Sheldon. *Politics and Vision: Continuity and Innovation in Western Political Thought.* Boston: Little, Brown & Co., 1960.

Publications from The Teaching of Ethics Project
The Hastings Center

A number of publications on the teaching of ethics in higher education are available from The Hastings Center. A list of these publications appears on the back cover. Return order form to: The Hastings Center, 360 Broadway, Hastings-on-Hudson, N.Y. 10706

I. **The Teaching of Ethics in Higher Education: A Report by The Hastings Center** . . . . ($5)
II. Michael J. Kelly, Legal Ethics and Legal Education . . . . ($4)
III. Clifford G. Christians & Catherine L. Covert, Teaching Ethics in Journalism Education . . . . ($4)
IV. K. Danner Clouser, Teaching Bioethics: Strategies, Problems, and Resources . . . . ($4)
V. Charles W. Powers & David Vogel, Ethics in the Education of Business Managers. . . . . ($5)
VI. Donald P. Warwick, The Teaching of Ethics in the Social Sciences. . . . . ($4)
VII. Robert J. Baum, Ethics and Engineering Curricula. . . . . ($4)
VIII. Joel L. Fleishman & Bruce L. Payne, Ethical Dilemmas and the Education of Policymakers . . . . ($4)
IX. Bernard Rosen & Arthur C. Caplan, Ethics in the Undergraduate Curriculum. ($4)

TOTAL COST _____

PRICES QUOTED ARE POSTPAID—
PREPAYMENT IS REQUIRED
There will be a $1 service charge
if billing is necessary.

Name _____

Address _____

City _____ State _____ Zip Code _____